CONTAINER
GARDENING

CONTAINER GARDENING

STEPHANIE DONALDSON

HERMES
HOUSE

This edition published by Hermes House in 2004

© Anness Publishing Limited 1997, 2004

Hermes House is an imprint of Anness Publishing Limited
Hermes House, 88–89 Blackfriars Road, London SE1 8HA

tel. 020 7401 2077; fax 020 7633 9499; info@anness.com

A CIP catalogue record for this book is available from the British Library.

Publisher: Joanna Lorenz
Project Editor: Fiona Eaton
Designer: Janet James
Photographers: Marie O'Hara,
Janine Hosegood, John Freeman
Stylist: Stephanie Donaldson

Previously published as *The Ultimate Container Gardener*

1 3 5 7 9 10 8 6 4 2

Contents

Introduction

Container gardening expands your horticultural horizon because it defies space and time. You do not need to be a full-time gardener with a large country garden to grow the lushest, tastiest herbs, wild strawberries, or white flowers for a summer evening.

The beauty of containers is that with the minimum amount of effort they will instantly jazz up a balcony or roof garden, extend the garden into an area of shady paving outside the back door and liven up window-sills with colour, scent and shape. They can also, of course, be used indoors. The range of possibilities is nothing short of amazing, even for gardeners who work on a large scale. The terraces at Powis Castle, for instance, a

medieval castle perched on a Welsh hillside, are famed for their elaborate, magical terracotta pots with the most flamboyant mix of plants. Containers add to the grace and majesty of even the grandest garden designs.

In the following pages you will find scores of imaginative themed ideas for beautiful containers with recommendations of some of the best plants around for achieving them. Don't be dismayed if you can't find exactly the plants suggested. There is nearly always an excellent alternative, and new varieties with brighter colours and bigger, longer-lasting blooms keep appearing in the nurseries. With a bit of experience, you'll soon be able to create your own eye-catching arrangements.

ABOVE: *Container gardening is a novel approach to creating your own miniature fruit and vegetable garden.*
RIGHT: *Plants are only part of the equation and decorative containers are readily available.*

The
Techniques

Types of Container

One of the challenges of container gardening is finding the right container for the right setting. You can now quite readily buy a whole range of lovely containers, for example, waist-high, Italian olive oil jars make a terrific focal point – big and bold and stylish. At the other end of the scale, you can be as imaginative as you like. You could use a Wellington boot or an old shoe for an engaging, quirky touch. In between, of course, the choice is huge: rustic terracotta, voguish metal or brightly painted tins, Mediterranean style.

It is important to consider the final setting when you are buying a container. A rustic tub may look charming under the window of a thatched cottage, but inappropriate outside a formal town house. Bear proportions in mind and, for example, choose a window box that exactly fits the sill. It is also worth noting that the weight of a container, when filled with compost and freshly watered, will be considerably greater than when empty. Think twice before packing your roof terrace or balcony with heavy pots: the structure may not be able to cope. And never leave a container on a window-sill from where it could fall down into the street.

Stone troughs

NOT SO READILY AVAILABLE BUT DEFINITELY WORTH LOOKING AT.
Advantages – durable and attractive.
Disadvantages – very heavy and expensive.

Pots and barrels

VERSATILE AND PRACTICAL.
Advantages – maintenance-free and versatile.
Disadvantages – heavy to move.

Wooden window boxes

GIVE A WOODEN CONTAINER AN ORIGINAL LOOK WITH YOUR OWN COLOUR SCHEME.
Advantages – you can change the look to suit any new planting scheme.
Disadvantages – the boxes require occasional maintenance.

Terracotta window boxes

AVAILABLE IN A WIDE RANGE OF SIZES AND STYLES.
Advantages – look good and appear even better with age.
Disadvantages – heavy, and may be damaged by frost.

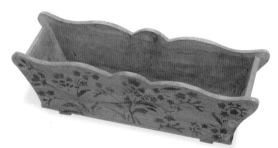

Types of Hanging Basket

Before you choose the plants and how to arrange them, decide what style of hanging basket you are going to display them in. Garden centres stock a huge variety, which are all easy to work with and hang. Hanging baskets are made from plastic-coated wire, wrought iron and galvanized wire. Plants can also look great trailing from window boxes.

Galvanized tin

TIN HAS MOVED FROM THE UTILITARIAN TO THE FASHIONABLE.

Advantages – an interesting variation from the usual materials.

Disadvantages – drainage holes required.

Lightweight fibre window boxes

PLAIN AND PRACTICAL.

Advantages – look rustic, and have a rich brown colour.

Disadvantages – short life-span.

Hanging baskets

VARIED AND PRACTICAL.

Advantages – look lovely planted.

Disadvantages – need to be lined before use.

Baskets

CAN BE USED AS WINDOW BOXES PROVIDED THEY ARE GENEROUSLY LINED WITH MOSS BEFORE PLANTING.

Advantages – lightweight and attractive.

Disadvantages – plant pots must be removed for watering, or the base of the basket will be soaked and rot.

Novelty containers

HUGELY UNDERRATED. USE ANYTHING FROM WATERING CANS OR TYRES TO SHOES.

Advantages – witty and fun.

Disadvantages – possible short life-span.

Propagation Techniques

Most containers and plants are available from garden centres but raising your own plants from seed or cuttings is far easier than you may think and can be very rewarding. Buying young plants from mail order catalogues is an increasingly popular way of starting a collection.

Seed Sowing

One of the cheapest ways of getting a mass planting is by growing plants from seed. It is fun, can be easy (when growing marigolds, for instance), and you don't need a high-tech greenhouse. Furthermore, if you get hooked on the plants, you can collect your own ripe seed in the autumn for a spring sowing the following year.

Cuttings

If you want to increase your stock of the plants you are already growing in the garden, you can get quick results by taking spring cuttings.

When the cuttings have rooted – this will be immediately obvious because they suddenly perk up – wait for the roots to fill the pot, and then transfer to individual pots.

1 Fill the seed tray with seed compost. Gently firm and level the surface by pressing down on the compost using a tray of the same size. When sowing large seeds, such as sunflowers or marigolds, use a dibber, cane or pencil to make holes for each seed. Plant the seeds and cover with compost.

2 When sowing small seeds they should be thinly scattered on the surface of the compost and then covered with just enough sieved sand and compost to conceal them. Firm the surface, using another tray. Water from above, using a fine rose on a watering can, or by standing the tray in water until the surface of the compost is moist.

1 Remove the new soft-wood growth when it is about 10 cm (4 in) long, just above a leaf node.

2 Using a sharp knife, trim the cutting just below a node and trim away the lower leaves.

3 Dip the end of the stem in hormone rooting powder, and plant up in a small container, using cuttings compost.

4 Fill the pot with cuttings, water, and place in a warm, bright place, out of scorching sunlight.

3 Enclose the seed tray in a plastic jar or bag to conserve moisture and cover with a black plastic bag, as most seeds germinate best in a warm dark place.

4 Check daily and bring into the light when the seedlings are showing.

5 To create a moist microclimate for the cuttings, it's a good idea to enclose the pot completely in a plastic bag. Secure it with an elastic band around the pot.

Mail Order

Send off each year for the latest seed and plant catalogues. You will invariably find a wider range than you can buy in a garden centre. Young plants are packed into special packages, which minimize damage during transit, but as they are restricted and in the dark they are initially weakened and some care is necessary to encourage vigorous growth.

1 Open the package with care. Leaves will probably unfold from the confined space. Each plant should be intact and clearly labelled.

2 Lift the plants out of their travelling box. Labels tucked underneath the root ball reduce the necessity for handling it directly and helps to keep the compost intact.

3 Plant in a small pot. If the plants seem very wilted, remove some of the larger leaves.

Potting On

After several weeks your young plants, whether grown from seed, mail order stock or cuttings, will need potting on. This simply means giving the young plant its own larger, individual container.

1 Young plants are ready to move into larger pots when the roots start to emerge through the holes in the base of the pot. Gently remove the rootball from the pot to check. If there is more than one seedling in the pot, carefully tease away each individual rootball. (Some plants hate to have their roots disturbed. The information on the seed packet will tell you this. These seeds are best sown individually in peat pots or modular trays.) Lower the rootball of the plant into a pot marginally bigger than the existing one.

2 Holding the plant carefully so as not to damage the stem, gently pour potting compost around the rootball, firming lightly.

3 Dibble the compost down the side of the pot to eliminate air spaces. It does not matter if the stem of the seedling is buried deeper than it was previously, as long as the leaves are well clear of the soil. Water, using a can with a fine rose.

Composts

Composts come in various formulations suitable for different plant requirements. A standard potting compost is usually peat-based and is suitable for all purposes. Peat and peat substitutes are relatively light in weight, and are therefore the obvious choice for hanging baskets. Regular watering is vital when using peat-based composts, as it is very difficult to moisten them again if they have been allowed to dry out completely. Different composts can be mixed together for specific plant needs.

Standard compost

The majority of composts available at garden centres are peat-based with added fertilizers.

Container compost

A peat-based compost with moisture-retaining granules and added fertilizer, specially formulated for window boxes and containers.

Ericaceous compost

A peat-based compost with no added lime, essential for rhododendrons, camellias and heathers in containers.

Peat-free compost

Manufacturers now offer a range of composts using materials from renewable resources such as coir fibre. They are used in the same way as peat-based composts.

Loam-based compost

Uses sterilized loam as the main ingredient, with fertilizers to supplement the nutrients in the loam. Although much heavier than peat-based compost, it can be lightened by mixing with peat-free compost. Ideal for long-term planting as it retains nutrients well.

THE ESSENTIAL FERTILIZER ELEMENTS

All plant fertilizers contain three key elements, nitrogen (N), phosphorous (P), and potassium/potash (K), with extra trace elements. These three promote, respectively, foliage growth, flower development, and fruit ripening and root development.

When buying a packet of fertilizer you can easily check the balance of the ingredients. It is printed as an "NPK" ratio, for instance 12:5:12. But don't be fooled into thinking that a reading of 24:10:24 is stronger, giving twice the value. It won't, of course, as the ratio is the same. A fertilizer with a ratio of 10:5:10 provides a sound, balanced diet. (You can purchase meters from garden centres that give a guide to the nutrient levels in the soil but they are not, to date, particularly accurate.)

Besides feeding, you can also trick some plants into a prolific display of flowering. Plants packed into small containers, with restricted (but not crippling) root space, feel that they are in danger of dying. Their immediate response is to do what all flowering plants are programmed to do – flower and set seed to continue the species.

Feeding Container Plants

It is not generally understood that most potting composts contain sufficient food for only six weeks of plant growth. After that, the plants will slowly starve unless more food is introduced. There are several products available, all of which are easy to use. Many of the projects in this book use slow-release plant food granules because they are the easiest and most reliable way of ensuring your plants receive sufficient food during the growing season. For these granules to be effective the compost needs to remain damp or the nutrients cannot be released.

Slow-release Plant Food Granules

These will keep your container plants in prime condition and are very easy to use. One application lasts six months, whereas most other plant foods need to be applied fortnightly. Follow the manufacturer's recommended dose carefully; additional fertilizer will simply leach away.

BELOW: *A variety of plant foods (clockwise from top left): liquid foliar feed, two types of pelleted slow-release plant food granules, a general fertilizer and loose slow-release plant food granules.*

TOP: *Slow-release plant food granules can be added to the compost or potting mix in the recommended quantity before filling the container and planting it.*

ABOVE: *When adding fertilizer granules to the soil, sprinkle them on to the surface of the compost and rake into the top layer. Pelleted granules should be pushed approximately 2 cm (3/4 in) below the surface.*

Watering Container Plants

Watering plants in containers is an acquired art, and an incredibly important one. You cannot leave it entirely to nature because rain tends to bounce off the leaves of the bushiest plants, soaking not into the pot but into the adjoining ground.

Outside, pot plants dry out very quickly on roasting hot days. Unlike plants in the ground, their roots are encircled by heat; some thirsty plants might even need two waterings a day, so keep checking. You have to get the balance right between over- and under-watering.

Trial and error is one way, but there are a few key tips, one of the best and simplest being to stick your finger deep into the soil to test for dryness. If you are unsure, wait until you see the first signs of wilting, then give the plant a thorough drink, letting the water drain out of the bottom of the pot. And always water plants either first thing in the morning or, better still, late at night, so that the moisture does not quickly evaporate. At all costs, try to avoid over-watering, which is a bigger killer than pests and diseases combined.

The best water is either rainwater or cold, boiled water, but it is not essential to use these unless your tap water is very hard, or you are growing lime-hating plants such as camellias. Don't allow your potted plants to become waterlogged. If there is any water remaining in the saucer half an hour after watering, tip it away.

Window Boxes and Pots

Don't rush the watering. Though you might think one soaking is enough for a big window box, it might only wet the top few inches of compost. Wait until the water sluices out of the bottom. Container composts include a water-retaining gel and if the compost remains wet in cold weather it can cause the roots to rot.

Hanging Baskets

Summer hanging baskets need daily watering even in overcast weather and on a hot day should be watered morning and evening. Once they have been allowed to dry out it can be difficult for the compost to re-absorb water. In these circumstances it is a good idea to immerse hanging baskets in a large bucket or bowl of water. Winter and spring hanging baskets should be watered only when the soil is dry.

LEFT: *Houseplants enjoy being sprayed with water, but in hard water areas you should use rainwater or bottled water.*

Water-retaining Gel

One of the main problems for most container gardeners is the amount of watering required to keep the plants thriving in the growing season. Adding water-retaining gels to compost will certainly help reduce this task. Sachets of gel are available from garden centres.

1 Pour the recommended amount of water into a bowl.

2 Scatter the gel over the surface, stirring occasionally until it has absorbed the water.

3 Add to your compost at the recommended rate, and mix the gel in thoroughly before using it for planting.

MULCHES

A mulch is a layer of protective material placed over the soil. It helps to retain moisture, conserve warmth, suppress weeds and prevent soil splash on foliage and flowers.

Bark chippings

Bark is an extremely effective mulch and as it rots down it conditions the soil. It works best when spread at least 7.5 cm (3 in) thick and is therefore not ideal for small containers. It is derived from renewable resources.

Clay granules

Clay granules are widely used for hydroculture, but can also be used to mulch houseplants. When placing a plant in a *cachepot*, fill all around the pot with granules. When watered, the granules absorb moisture, which is then released slowly to create a moist microclimate for the plant.

Gravel

Gravel makes a decorative mulch for container plants, and also provides the correct environment for plants such as alpines. It is available in a variety of sizes and colours which can be matched to the scale and colours of the plants used.

Stones

Smooth stones can be used as decorative mulch for large container-grown plants. You can save stones dug out of the garden, collect your own from beaches and riverbeds or buy stones from garden centres. They also deter cats from using the soil as a litter tray.

Pests and Diseases

Container plants are every bit as susceptible to aphid and slug attacks as those grown in the garden. But they are generally easier to keep an eye on, so the moment you see a pest attack, take action. Most pests multiply at a staggering rate, and once a plant has been vigorously assaulted, it takes a long time to recover.

Common Pests

Aphids

These sap-sucking insects feed on the tender growing tips. Most insecticides are effective against aphids such as greenfly or blackfly (shown above). Choose one that will not harm ladybirds.

Mealy bugs

These look like spots of white mould. They are hard to shift and regular treatment with a systemic insecticide is the best solution.

Caterpillars

The occasional caterpillar can be picked off the plant and disposed of as you see fit, but a major infestation can strip a plant before your eyes. Contact insecticides are usually very effective.

Red spider mite

An insect that thrives indoors in dry conditions. Constant humidity will reduce the chance of an infestation, which is indicated by the presence of fine webs and mottling of the plant's leaves. To treat an infestation, pick off the worst affected leaves and spray the plants with an insecticide.

Vine weevils

These white grubs are a menace. The first sign of an infestation is the sudden collapse of the plant because the weevil has eaten its roots. Systemic insecticides or natural predators can be used as a preventative, but once a plant has been attacked it is usually too late to save it. Never re-use the soil from an affected plant. The picture above shows an adult weevil.

Snails

Snails cannot generally reach hanging baskets, but are more of a problem in wall baskets and window boxes: they tuck themselves behind the container during daylight and venture out to feast at night. Use slug pellets or venture out yourself with a torch and catch them.

Whitefly

These tiny white flies flutter up in clouds when disturbed from their feeding places on the undersides of leaves. Whitefly are particularly troublesome in conservatories, where a dry atmosphere will encourage them to breed. Keep the air as moist as possible. Contact insecticides will need more than one application to deal with an infestation, but a systemic insecticide will protect the plant for weeks.

Common Diseases

Black spot – most commonly seen on roses; dark spots on leaves occur before they fall. Burn all affected foliage, and treat with a fungicide.
Botrytis – immediately evident as a pernicious, furry grey mould. Remove and burn all affected parts, and treat with a fungicide.
Powdery mildew – most likely to affect potted fruit trees. Remove and burn affected parts. Treat with a fungicide.
Rust – high humidity causes orange/dark brown pustules on the stem. Remove and burn affected parts. Treat with a fungicide.
Viruses (various) – the varied symptoms include distorted, mis-shapen leaves, and discoloration. Vigorous anti-aphid controls are essential. Destroy affected foliage.

Pest Control

There are three main types of pest control available to combat common pests.

Systemic insecticides

These work by being absorbed by the plant's root or leaf system, and killing insects that come into contact with the plant. This will work for difficult pests, such as the grubs of vine weevils which are hidden in the soil, and scale insects which protect themselves from above with a scaly cover.

Biological control

Commercial growers now use biological control in their glasshouses; this means natural predators are introduced to eat the pest population. Although not all are suitable for the amateur gardener, they can be used in conservatories for dealing with pests such as whitefly.

Contact insecticides

These must be sprayed directly on to the insects to be effective. Most organic insecticides work this way, but they generally kill all insects, even beneficial ones, such as hoverflies and ladybirds. Try to remove these before spraying the infected plant.

NATURAL PREDATORS

Aphidius – a wasp that lays eggs in young aphids; on hatching they devour the host.
Aphidoletes – a gall midge that devours aphids.
Bacillus thuringinesis – a bacterium that kills caterpillars.
Cryptolaemus montrouzieri – an Australian ladybird that eats mealy bug. It is activated by a temperature of 20°C (68°F).
Encarsia formosa – a parasitic wasp that lays eggs in the larvae of whitefly. The young wasps eat their hosts.

Metaphycus – a parasitic wasp, activated by a temperature of 20°C (68°F), that kills off soft scales.
Phasmarhabditis – a nematode that kills slugs provided the temperature of the soil is above 5°C (41°F).
Phytoseiulus persimilis – attacks red spider mite provided the temperature is 20°C (68°F).
Steinernema – kills vine weevils by releasing a bacterium into them. Needs a temperature of 12°C (53°F).

Suitable Container Plants

Annuals and Biennials

Whether you raise them yourself from seed in the greenhouse or on the kitchen window-sill, or buy them in strips from the garden centre for an instant effect, fast-growing annuals and biennials will quickly and cheaply fill baskets and boxes and flower prolifically all summer to produce eye-catching effects. Choose compact varieties that will not need support. Trailing annuals such as lobelia, nasturtiums and dwarf sweet peas are all invaluable for hanging baskets. Some perennial species, including petunias, pelargoniums and busy Lizzies (impatiens), are normally grown as annuals.

Tender Perennials

Beautiful tender and half-hardy plants such as osteospermums, verbenas, pelargoniums, petunias and fuchsias are ideal for containers, where their showy flowers can be fully appreciated. Raise new plants from cuttings for next season. If you buy young, tender plants from the garden centre in the spring, don't be tempted to put newly planted boxes or baskets outside until all danger of frost is past.

ABOVE: *Trailing nasturtiums make a glorious display, providing colour from early summer.*

LEFT: *Petunias and pelargoniums are tender perennials, which are often grown as annuals.*

BELOW: *Containers of spring bulbs such as these yellow tulips cannot fail to delight.*

Evergreen Perennials

Evergreen non-woody perennials such as ajugas, bergenias and *Carex oshimensis* 'Evergold' are always useful for providing colour and foliage in the winter, but look best as part of a mixed planting.

For single plantings, try *Agapanthus africanus* or *A. orientalis* with their blue flowers on tall stems. For a more architectural shape, consider one of the many different eryngiums (sea holly). *E. agavifolium* is particularly attractive, and has greenish-white flowers in late summer.

Border Perennials

Few people bother to grow perennials in containers, but if you have a paved garden, or would like to introduce them to the patio, don't be afraid to experiment. Dicentras, agapanthus, and many ornamental grasses are among the plants that you might want to try, but there are very many more that you should be able to succeed with – and they will cost you nothing if you divide a plant already in the border.

Bulbs

Bulbs, particularly the spring varieties make ideal container plants. Bulbs should be planted at twice the depth of their own length. They can be packed in as tight as you like, and even in layers, so that you get a repeat-showing after the first display. Note that when planting lilies (the white, scented, fail-safe *Lilium regale* is a fine choice if you have never tried them before), they need excellent drainage, so put in an extra layer of grit at the bottom. And to prevent spearing the bulb later on with a plant support, insert this in the compost at the same time.

Shrubs for Tubs

Camellias are perfect shrubs for tubs, combining attractive, glossy evergreen foliage with beautiful spring flowers. *Camellia* x *williamsii* and *C. japonica* hybrids are a good choice. Many rhododendrons and azaleas are also a practical proposition, and if you have a chalky soil this is the best way to grow these plants – provided you fill the container with an ericaceous compost.

Many hebes make good container plants (but not for very cold or exposed areas), and there are many attractively variegated varieties. The yellow-leaved *Choisya ternata* 'Sundance' and variegated yuccas such as *Yucca filamentosa* 'Variegata' and *Y. gloriosa* 'Variegata' are also striking shrubs for containers.

For some winter interest, try *Viburnum tinus*.

Topiary for Pots

Topiarized box is ideal for a pot. However, it is relatively slow growing at about 30 cm (12 in) a year. It may be best to buy a mature, ready-shaped plant, although you miss the fun of doing the pruning.

ABOVE: *If your garden cannot support lime-hating rhododendrons, do not despair. They can easily be grown in pots, in ericaceous compost, giving colour from autumn, through winter, to summer.*

LEFT: *Pots on plinths and fruit trees in tubs create a marvellous architectural effect, with plenty of striking verticals.*

Trees for Tubs

Trees are unlikely candidates for containers, particularly for small gardens. Fortunately, the restricted root-run usually keeps them compact and they never reach the proportions of trees planted in the ground. Even in a small garden, some height is useful.

Choose trees that are naturally small if possible. Laburnums, crab apples (and some of the upright-growing and compact eating apples on dwarfing rootstocks), *Prunus* 'Amanogawa' (a flowering cherry with narrow, upright growth), and even trees as potentially large as *Acer platanoides* 'Drummondii' (a variegated maple) will be happy in a large pot or tub for a number of years. Small weeping trees also look good. Try *Salix caprea pendula* or *Cotoneaster* 'Hybridus Pendulus' (which has cascades of red berries in autumn). Even the pretty dome-shaped, grey-leaved *Pyrus salicifolia* 'Pendula' is a possibility.

These must have a heavy pot with a minimum inside diameter of 38 cm (15 in), and a loam-based compost. Even then they are liable to blow over in very strong winds unless you pack some other hefty pots around them during stormy weather.

Planting Pots

Planting up a container of any size could not be easier, as long as you follow a few basic rules. First, terracotta pots need a layer of material at the bottom to help the water drain away quickly. Plastic pots usually have sufficient drainage holes. Second, always plant into the appropriate size pot; that is, slightly larger than the rootball. Putting a small plant into a large pot is counter productive. The plant will put on good root growth at the expense of flowers and foliage. Since the hungry root system will drink up water rapidly in summer, check regularly that the soil is not too dry.

ABOVE: *Beautiful, elegant urns do not always need the finest flowering plants. As these twin pots show, even a modest planting works well. Indeed, it is often preferable because it does not detract from the gorgeous containers.*

Maintaining Plants

Large plants can grow in surprisingly small containers. They will not grow to the same height as if they were given a free root run, but should be impressive nonetheless. If possible, remove the top layer of soil every year, and replace it with fresh compost. There comes a time, however, when most plants finally outgrow their containers. What then? You can replace the mature plant with a cutting and start again. Alternatively, stick instead to plants that are slow-growing, or which will not rapidly fill their pots with roots. Or root prune.

Root pruning is a remarkably easy technique, which involves removing the plant from the pot in spring, when it is beginning to put on good growth. Either slice away the exterior of the rootball quite boldly, or snip at it with secateurs. Then replace in the existing pot, filling the gap with fresh compost.

Overwintering

Remember that while tender plants may just survive winter outside in your area, with their roots protected deep below ground, those in pots are much less likely to survive. The roots will be just the width of the pot (a few centimetres) away from encircling snow or icy winds. Bring these plants indoors or, if you do not have room, take cuttings before the end of the season.

Planting in Terracotta

Terracotta containers are always popular, but need some preparation before planting.

1 With terracotta it is essential to provide some form of drainage material in the base of the container. When planting in large pots or boxes, recycle broken-up polystyrene plant trays as drainage material. Lumps of polystyrene are excellent for this purpose and as they retain warmth they are of additional benefit to the plant.

2 In smaller pots the drainage material can be broken pieces of pot, known as crocks, or gravel.

Planting in Plastic

When buying plastic pots or boxes, check that the drainage holes are open. Some manufacturers mark the holes but leave it to the purchaser to punch or drill them out as required.

Plant Supports

Climbing plants in containers will need support. This can be provided by one or more canes which are pushed into the pot, a free-standing plant frame or a trellis fastened to a wall behind the container.

Planting in Wicker Baskets

If you wish to use a more unconventional container as a window box you may need to seal it with a sheet of plastic to prevent leakage.

1 Line the basket with a generous layer of moss which will prevent the compost leaking away.

2 Fill the basket with compost, and mix in plant food granules or any organic alternative you wish to use.

Saucers and Feet

Saucers are available for plastic and clay pots. They act as water reservoirs for the plants, and are used under houseplants to protect the surface they are standing on. Clay saucers must be fully glazed if they are used indoors or they will leave marks. Clay feet are available for terracotta pots. They will prevent the pot becoming waterlogged, but this also means that in a sunny position the pot will dry out very quickly and may need extra watering.

Plastic plant saucers can be used to line and protect containers which are not waterproof, such as this wooden apple-basket.

Hanging Gardens

When you want colour high up or relating closely to the building, the easiest way is to create a hanging garden, either in baskets or in wall-mounted containers. A purpose-made hanging basket is designed so that as the flowers grow, they cascade through the side and spill over the edge in a joyous show of colour, covering the whole basket. An alternative is to make the basket or container part of the display. Ordinary shopping baskets, buckets, agricultural containers, even kitchen equipment such as colanders, pots and pans, can be used.

Planting and Positioning Hanging Baskets

One hanging basket, alone on a wall, can look rather insignificant. Far better to plant up baskets in pairs, either with similar plants to create an echoing effect, or with clashing, contrasting colours. For a really stunning effect, entirely cover a wall with baskets, but remember that they are very demanding, and will need prolific watering in a dry mid-summer.

If the container is large and in danger of getting too heavy for its support, one trick is to put a layer of broken-up expanded polystyrene (from plant trays or electrical goods packaging) in the bottom of the container. This is lighter than the equivalent amount of compost and provides good drainage. Containers should have drainage holes, and baskets will need lining to stop the soil from being washed out while you are watering. Liners can be home-made from pieces of plastic sheet cut to size, with a layer of moss tucked between the basket and plastic for a more decorative look. Alternatively, you can use a proprietary liner, made from paper pulp, to fit purpose-made hanging baskets, or coconut matting – which comes in a variety of shapes and sizes to adapt to all kinds of baskets.

Whichever type of container you choose, it needs to be filled with a good compost, and adding fertilizer granules and water-retaining gel can also help promote lush results and make care and maintenance a little easier.

RIGHT: *Hanging baskets filled with pansies create a lovely focal point of gentle colour.*

Preparing Hanging Baskets

The key to successful hanging baskets is in the preparation. Time taken in preparing the basket for planting will be rewarded with a long-lasting colourful display. Slow-release plant food granules incorporated into the compost when planting ensure that the plants receive adequate nutrients throughout the growing season. It is essential to water hanging baskets every day, even in overcast weather, as they dry out very quickly. There are various ways to line a hanging basket.

Choosing a Lining

1 When buying a hanging basket, make sure that the chains are detachable. By unhooking one of the chains, they can be placed to one side of the basket, allowing you to work freely. Either rest the basket on a flat surface, or sit it on a flowerpot.

2 Traditionally, hanging baskets are lined with sphagnum moss. This looks very attractive and plants can be introduced at any point in the side of the basket. As sphagnum moss tends to dry out rather faster than other liners, it is advisable to use a compost containing water-retaining gel with this lining.

3 Coir fibre liners are a practical substitute for moss. Although not as good to look at, the coir will soon be hidden as the plants grow. The slits in the liner allow for planting in the side of the basket.

4 Cardboard liners are clean and easy to use. They are made in various sizes to fit most hanging baskets.

5 Press out the marked circles on the cardboard liner if you wish to plant into the side of the basket.

Underplanting a Hanging Basket

Underplanting helps to achieve a really lush-looking basket and soon conceals the shape of the container under flowers and foliage.

1 Line the lower half of the basket with a generous layer of moss.

2 Rest the rootball on the moss and gently guide the foliage through the side of the basket.

3 Add more moss to the basket, tucking it carefully around the plants to ensure that they are firmly in place. Add a further row of plants near the top edge of the basket, if required, and continue to line the basket with moss, finishing off with a collar of moss overlapping the rim of the basket. Fill with compost.

Year-round Containers

Containers are traditionally used for creating extra, lavish colourful effects in summer. With a little thought and careful planning you can enjoy delightful containers all year round.

First Signs of Spring

Early spring bulbs burst into life as soon as winter loosens its grip. Even on chilly, rainy days, pots planted with small bulbs – snowdrops, crocuses, scillas and *Iris reticulata* – will provide splashes of clear colour on the patio or window-sills, and can be briefly brought indoors, if you like, for an early taste of spring. Primulas and polyanthus look great in containers, too. If you grow lily-of-the-valley in the garden, pot up a few roots and bring them inside: they'll come into bloom weeks early.

ABOVE AND LEFT: *Plants might not flourish in the garden border all year round, but you can still have some delightful plants every day of the year. Here, small pots of lily-of-the-valley, dwarf irises, crocuses and primroses brighten up a warm day in early spring.*

Summer Blooms

Summer is, of course, the highlight of the container gardener's year, giving the opportunity for lovely creative plantings. Deciding which plants to use is an enjoyable task.

RIGHT: *For a really eye-catching container, be different. A large potted mix, featuring summer bedding plants topped by a lanky white fuchsia, is encircled by a rustic woven sheep feeder. The effect is heightened by tufts of grass packed into the gaps.*

FAR RIGHT: *A flamboyant show of billowing annuals.*

Autumn Highlights

Grow one or two autumn-glory shrubs in tubs that you can bring out when you need a final burst of colour on the patio.

Ceratostigma willmottiamum has compact growth and lovely autumn foliage tints while still producing blue flowers. Berries can also be used as a feature, and you can usually buy compact gaultherias already bearing berries in your garden centre.

ABOVE: *Potted chrysanthemums (here flanked by ericas) are an easy and excellent way of prolonging bright summer colours into autumn.*

Winter Colour

Some winter-flowering shrubs can be used in tubs, such as *Viburnum tinus* and *Mahonia x media* 'Charity'. Try being bold with short-term pot plants such as Cape heathers (*Erica hyemalis* and *E. gracilis*) and winter cherries (*Solanum capsicastrum* and similar species and hybrids). You will have to throw them away afterwards, but they will look respectable for a few weeks even in cold and frosty winter weather.

HOW TO PROTECT PLANTS FROM FROST

Many of the most dramatic summer patio shrubs – like daturas and oleanders – must be taken into a frost-free place for the winter. Others that are frost-tolerant but of borderline hardiness in cold areas, like the bay (*Laurus nobilis*), or that are vulnerable to frost and wind damage to the leaves (such as *Choisya ternata* 'Sundance') need a degree of winter protection. It is a pity to lose these magnificent patio plants for the sake of a little forethought as autumn draws to a close. Shrubs that are fairly tough and need a little protection from the worst weather can be covered with horticultural fleece, or bubbly polythene. If you use fleece, you may be able to buy it as a sleeve (ideal for winter protection for shrubs in tubs).

1 Insert four or five canes around the edge of the pot. Cut the polythene to size. Allow for an overlap over the pot.

2 Wrap it around the plant, allowing a generous overlap. For particularly vulnerable plants, use more than one layer. Securely tie the protection around the pot. For very delicate plants, bring the material well down over the pot, to keep the rootball warm. Leave the top open for ventilation and to permit watering if necessary.

GARDENER'S TIP

If covering with fleece, tie the top together (moisture will be able to penetrate, and tying the top will help to conserve warmth).

OPPOSITE: *Smooth, topiarized box balls and pyramids catch the eye at any time of year. You can buy them ready styled or, better still, raise your own cuttings and shape them as you wish.*

Colour-theme Plantings

Create impact in the garden by colour-theming seasonal planting to tune in with their surroundings. This works best with plants in containers as the containers can be chosen to tone and blend with the walls, then planted with flowers in complementary colours. Once the blooms are over, they can be replaced by new plantings for the next season. You do not always have to match the colours; you may decide to use contrasting colours instead. In this way, the garden looks fresh and bright all year round and you have several scene changes to enjoy as the seasons pass.

ABOVE: *The blue-green and purple tones of ornamental cabbage look fabulous in a galvanized grey bucket, set against the blue-green of a painted fence.*

OPPOSITE: *An orange-yellow poppy and cream-coloured violas look stunning planted in beige pots, set against the warm ochre shades of a brick wall.*

ABOVE: *This pot has been painted in stripes to link the green background and pink blooms of a wonderful hebe.*

Colour-splash Plantings

Just as you can decorate the inside of your home with colourful flower arrangements, so you can do the same outside. Use pots of flowering plants to provide a colourful splash in a prominent part of the garden or to decorate the outdoor living area when entertaining. Create an immediate colour impact by choosing a colour theme and teaming containers and plants in toning shades. Try painting some terracotta pots specially to match your favourite flowers. You could also make a tablescape for a special occasion, using a variety of containers and seasonal flowering plants in hot clashing colours or in cool shades of blue, purple and white.

ABOVE: *Simple and magical, it is as though the rich colouring of the tulips has leaked out of the petals and dripped down the side of the pots.*

ABOVE: *Even a couple of ordinary terracotta garden pots hanging on the wall make interesting decorative detail, especially when they are both planted with a froth of white blooms.*

LEFT: *The papery white flowers of the petunias are underplanted with white lobelia and surrounded by silver Helichrysum. The basket looks wonderful in the pale light of a summer's evening.*

ABOVE: *Bright, bold, hothouse colours are very effective in groups.*
Try to find equally brightly coloured planters and containers.

Creating Cameo Gardens

If you are lucky enough to have a spare part of the garden where nothing is going on, liven it up by introducing a set theme. It can be witty and original, or have a theme to merge with the rest of the garden. Or it could even be a special private area packed with all your favourite pots.

Cameo gardens can provide a surprise in a small corner, embellish an under-used area or even provide a miniature project for children, who love to have a space of their own. The idea is to find a theme – herbs, perhaps, or pansies, miniature vegetables or lavender – then make up a "sampler", providing a different container for each variety. Alternatively, you can make the containers the

theme, choosing watering cans, culinary pots, pans and colanders, enamelware or terracotta in different shapes and sizes. Another idea is to design a miniature formal garden, perhaps taking inspiration from the classic Italian style. Choose a piece of small statuary as a focal point, then clip some young box plants into a miniature hedge surround and fill in with dwarf lavender.

LEFT: *For a seaside-type garden, use a stone-coloured pot and grey-leaved plants to blend in with the sandy background.*

Pots for Privacy

To be able to relax totally in the garden, you need to satisfy two basic requirements: privacy and shelter. Without the benefit of enclosed spaces, especially in built-up areas, these considerations can be problematic. However, there are ways of achieving them. Trellis can be fixed on top of walls and fences to create extra height. You can then grow decorative climbers to provide a wonderful natural wallpaper. And within this enclosure you can create a special atmosphere with the use of gorgeous pots. In fact, pots score over plants in beds because they can be swapped round with other containers in the rest of the garden, giving a constant change of scenery.

One way of conveying privacy is by furnishing this area like a real room. A row of shelves for a collection of, say, pelargoniums, pouring out rich red and magenta flowers and subtler hues. Verbenas make an

excellent alternative, and can either be left to tumble, or trained up miniature wigwams of green sticks to provide a side-show in blues, mauves and purples, interspersed with white. Violas are equally small-scale and domestic, with the added advantage that, being placed at eye level, their amazingly exquisite, detailed patterning can be fully appreciated. But perhaps the best container plants for outdoor shelving, or even an old, brightly painted open kitchen display unit, are auricula primulas.

Auriculas impart a strong Victorian feel (although they were actually introduced in the late 16th century) with their ornate faces, which are so exquisite that they used to be displayed inside an empty picture frame. One by itself is always an eye-catcher, leaving the viewer demanding more. Visit a specialist nursery to see a wide range.

Scented Pots

An enclosed area with no wind is the perfect place to grow scented pot plants where the perfume can hang in the air. You can have anything from marzipan to the smell of melting, rich brown chocolate. Just place the pots around a chair, sit back and relax.

Daphne odora 'Aureomarginata' makes a perfect shrub for a tub. It grows quite slowly to about 1.5m (5ft), and has purplish flowers, and the most ravishing scent imaginable. Feed well, place in the sun, and add plenty of grit to the soil for quick drainage.

Jasminum officinale is a fast, vigorous climber; it will quickly race up the side of a house or, with a restricted root run, can be trained round a large frame. Give it a hot sunny spot, water well, and inhale. Lilies have equally strong scents. The range is huge, running from the highly popular and reliable *Lilium regale* to the various, multi-coloured hybrids like 'Black Dragon' and 'Green Dragon', to the stunning strain called Imperial Crimson, with white flowers speckled red. Good drainage is the secret of success.

For a talking point, choose the unusual but wonderful *Cosmos atrosanguineus* which has dark maroon flowers and a whiff of chocolate on hot, sunny days. For marzipan, try an old-fashioned heliotrope like 'Princess Marina'. And for an unusual small black flower and the scent of summer fruits, plant up *Salvia discolor*.

RIGHT: *Thyme-filled gardens have a distinguished history, and have been popular since the medieval period. The trick is to choose a selection, with round and needle-like leaves, to create a rich tapestry in shades of green, gold and silver.*

Novel Themes

Edible gardens are always popular, and besides growing potted fruit trees and strawberries, it is worth experimenting with different kinds of salad. Lettuces now come in a wide range of shapes and colours and the more ornamental forms of herbs like basil and sage are just as delicious as the green varieties.

You can also grow a range of potted plants with different textured foliage. Smooth and svelte, sharp and pointed, rubbery and mounded, are all available. When next visiting a garden centre, do not just go in with your eyes open but with a stroking, extended hand. Plants appeal to more senses than one.

ABOVE: *A marvellous concoction made from the simplest of easily gathered materials. A scattering of wet beach pebbles frames a circular pattern, backed up by a group of small pots and chimney pots, planted with a wide selection of succulents.*

TOP: *Serried ranks of watering cans in the soft greys of weathered, galvanized metal make a beautiful feature in themselves. Planted up with hostas and violas, they become a highly original cameo garden.*

ABOVE: *This terracotta garden is focused around tall, long-tom pots planted with hostas, ivies and clematis let loose so that it behaves like a trailer, rather than a climber. Old drain covers and edging tiles add character.*

LEFT: *Potted plants always give plenty of impact when arranged in groups and one way to display them is on old baker's shelves in rows and rows of pots.*

RIGHT: *Themed gardens do not come much better than this. A sensational group of battered, wizened old boots double up as containers. The sumptuous profusion of pelargoniums in full blast obviously couldn't be happier.*

Potted Table Decorations

Outdoor table decorations are easy to put together and are at their most successful when they complement their surroundings. Simply gather together some of the smaller pots from around the garden, you may plunder the garden for a few cut flowers or foliage to add, or even add fruit and vegetables to complete the effect. The concentration in one place of what grows in naturally looser arrangements throughout the garden focuses the overall look.

BELOW: *Spring narcissi are perfectly in scale for a table setting. And with so many varieties having strong scents, there's nowhere better to appreciate them while relaxing over a long cold drink?*

RIGHT: *Ornamental cabbages, complemented by individual cabbage leaves used decoratively on the napkins and a miniature arrangement in a small jar, make an unusual centrepiece.*

BELOW: *A wire basket with raffia interwoven round its base gathers together pots of verbena surrounded by tiny pots of variegated ivy. The end result is an outdoor casualness perfectly in accord with its surroundings.*

LEFT: *In summer, a couple of potted strawberry plants are transformed into an original decoration when arranged in a wire jug with some extra ripe fruits.*

Location Plantings

Finding the right place for the right plant is the key to successful container gardening. One way of tackling the problem is to see container plants as a way of extending the garden into areas where plants do not normally grow. Once you have made a list of such areas, and it is always far longer than you would initially imagine, decide which kind of plants you would like growing there – climbers, scented plants, or plants to screen unsightly areas.

BELOW: *A classical, clipped, mop-head bay tree* (Laurus nobilis) *makes a smart entrance, and adds to the sense of formality. Its geometric shape is cleverly offset by a massed underplanting of lovely pink-flowering fuchsias.*

RIGHT: *An excellent way of livening up a typical suburban porch. Tropical, strap-shaped leaves add height and structure to a mass of smaller evergreens.*

Entrance Containers

A bare porch can be made to look far more welcoming and attractive by the addition of one large plant in a pot or urn. In warm, sheltered parts of the country you could try growing an exotic scented plant like one of the more tender daphnes (eg the evergreen *D. bholua* 'Jacqueline Postill') in a bright, south-facing spot.

If space is limited, you could hang smaller, ornate terracotta pots on the wall, one above the other, each with attractive, trailing growth. Or fix one or two hanging baskets just outside the porch, to provide aerial colour. But if you live in a particularly cold area, stick to summer bedding plants in the growing season, and for the rest of the year be content with one large, attractive urn. Even when unfilled, it can still be quite a feature.

Containers for Corners

Bare corners are all too often taken for granted, a kind of necessary evil. But there is no reason why they cannot add to the garden's glamour. Corners that are paved or covered with stony shingle make the perfect stage for a group of pots whose foliage and flowers mix and mingle, creating striking effects.

The key principle is to place the smaller plants at the front where they can be seen, with the medium-high plants behind, and the tallest at the back. Alternatively, choose a small group of elegant containers, using the plants in a more restrained way. A trailer growing from a pedestal container with a cluster of distinctive smaller plants round the base can be as stunning as a large group.

BELOW: *Antique stone urns like this are ideal for sharp corners where they both create a special feature and help soften a stark 90° angle with curves, colour and interest.*

1 This shady area next to a driveway has been gravelled to break up the effect of a large area of paving but still looks bleak and uninteresting.

2 Plants in containers have transformed this corner. Even though the plants may not completely conceal the wires and downpipe, there is now so much else to interest the eye that they are easily overlooked.

Pots for Steps and Walls

Steps and wall tops are too often left bare when they actually make a perfect platform for a row of colourful pot plants. The outside steps rising up to the top floor of a barn, for example, like a series of rising plinths, make a perfect stage for a series of pot plants, each tumbling colour on to the step below.

ABOVE LEFT: *The severe, formal Georgian entrance to this town house is wonderfully softened by the use of a row of containers on a ledge, packed with white-flowering fuchsias. Note how they complement the colour scheme.*

ABOVE: *Miniature violas, one plant to a pot, make an enchanting decoration for old stone steps.*

1 This terrace of old brick and stone is attractive in its own right, but is not as colourful as it might be.

2 The addition of a variety of containers with flowering plants completes the picture and adds colour and depth to the scene.

Containers as Screens, and with Arbours and Arches

Where you have a garden eyesore, such as a crumbling outhouse or drainage pipe, use ingenuity and imagination to hide it. You do not need to go overboard. A large pot containing a prolific marguerite (argyranthemum) will produce hundreds of daisy-like blooms all summer. You could even grow this plant as a standard, with a mop-head of growth on a 90cm (3ft) high single stem. A planted container, whether hanging or on the ground, is a lovely finishing touch to a garden arch or arbour.

TOP: *This arbour would look very bare without its glorious hanging basket of petunias.*

ABOVE: *A pair of formal containers planted with fuchsia standards, complement this garden archway perfectly.*

LEFT: *A colourful window box is used here to mark the edge of a border.*

Decorating
Containers

One of the joys of container gardening is decorating your own pots,
giving them exactly the right colour scheme to suit the plants and their surroundings.
Decorating pots is an undervalued and under-explored art. The majority of
plant pots sold in garden centres are plain brown, which people assume is the
colour they have to be. As the following projects show, plant pots are like
empty canvases. You can turn them into bright, colourful containers
with a Mediterranean feel, or much subtler pots in the softest of tones. It is also worth
experimenting with more unusual containers such as tin cans and buckets.

ABOVE: *Terracotta pots decorated with simple geometric shapes in*
yellow and green make perfect containers for spring bulbs.

44

Tin Can Plant Nursery

Seedlings can be decorative in themselves, so prick them out from their seed trays into a collection of shiny aluminium cans mounted on to a plaque. They can grow there until they are ready to be planted out. The plaque itself looks wonderful made from ordinary aluminium cans, but if you want to add a bit more colour, scour the shelves of delicatessens for some unusual printed cans and enjoy some culinary treats at the same time.

MATERIALS

Piece of board, about   Metal snippers
  60 x 30 cm (24 x 12 in) Pliers
Undercoat   Nail
Coloured gloss paint   Hammer
Decorating brush   Tin tacks
Can opener
Variety of empty
  aluminium cans with
  the labels removed

1 Apply an undercoat followed by a coat of gloss paint to the board, allowing each coat to dry completely.

2 Use the can opener to remove the top of each can if this has not already been done. Wash out the cans thoroughly.

3 Using metal snippers, cut down the side of each can and cut off half of the bottom.

4 Open out the sides with pliers and snip a V-shape into each one. Pierce the bottom of each can, using a nail and hammer.

5 Try out the arrangement of the cans on the board. Then, using one tin tack at each side point of the cans, nail into position.

Mexican Painted Pots

A series of traditional folk-art motifs painted over stripes of vibrant colours gives simple pots a rich Mexican look. Enhance the effect by allowing some of the untreated terracotta colour to show through, especially if you use pots with a fluted top like this one. Planted up with pelargoniums in hot summer colours, and stacked together, they make a lively garden feature.

MATERIALS

Terracotta pot with fluted-top
Masking tape
White undercoat
Small decorating brush
Artist's gouache paints
Fine and medium artist's brushes
Polyurethane matt varnish

1 Mark the stripes on the pot using masking tape. Cut some lengths into narrower widths to get variation in the finished design. Bear in mind that the areas covered by masking tape will remain natural terracotta.

2 Paint the body of the pot with undercoat, avoiding the fluted rim. Allow to dry completely.

3 Paint the coloured stripes with gouache paints, changing colour after each band of masking tape. Allow to dry completely.

4 Peel off the masking tape to reveal coloured stripes alternating with terracotta stripes.

5 Using the fine artist's brush and white undercoat, paint simple motifs over the stripes. When completely dry, coat with matt varnish.

Verdigris Bucket

There is something irresistible about the luminous, blue-green tones of verdigris. It is a colour that always complements plants and is not difficult to reproduce on a cheap galvanized bucket. To make the rust bucket shown behind the verdigris one, follow the steps below, but substitute rust-coloured acrylic paint for the aqua paint.

MATERIALS

Galvanized bucket
Medium-grade sandpaper
Metal primer
Small decorating brush
Gold paint
Amber shellac
Artist's acrylic paint in white and aqua-green
Water for mixing
Natural sponge
Polyurethane matt varnish

1 Sand the bucket, then prime with metal primer. Allow to dry for 2–3 hours. Paint with gold paint and allow to dry for 2–3 hours.

2 Paint with amber shellac and allow to dry for 30 minutes. Mix white acrylic paint with aqua-green and enough water to make a liquid consistency.

3 Sponge on the verdigris paint and allow to dry for 1–2 hours. Apply a coat of varnish.

Lead Chimney

The wonderful chalky tones of lead have made it a popular material for garden containers down the centuries. However, lead is incredibly heavy and very expensive, so here is a way of faking it, using a plastic, terracotta-coloured chimney and some simple paint effects.

MATERIALS

Plastic, terracotta-
  coloured chimney
Sandpaper
Acrylic primer
Large artist's brush

Emulsion (latex) paint in
  charcoal grey and white
Acrylic scumble glaze
Water
Decorating brush
Polyurethane matt varnish

1 Sand the chimney to give it a key. Paint with one coat of acrylic primer and allow to dry for 1–2 hours.

2 Apply one coat of charcoal-grey emulsion and allow to dry for 2–3 hours.

3 Tint the scumble glaze with white emulsion and thin with water. Paint over the chimney randomly. Wash over with water and allow to dry.

4 Add more of the white scumble mixture to parts of the chimney for extra colour and "age". Varnish with polyurethane matt varnish when dry.

A Shell Window Box

Decorated window boxes provide a delightful finish to windows, almost bringing the garden into the house. Being flat-fronted, they are also easier to decorate than round pots. Here, mussel shells lend impact to a co-ordinated planting of lavender and violas. Experiment with different shapes, using some mussel shells face-up and others face-down.

MATERIALS

Small terracotta window box
Mussel shells
Glue gun and all-purpose glue
  sticks
Crocks or pebbles
Compost
Water-retaining gel
Slow-release plant food granules
2 lavender plants
Tray of young viola plants

1 When you are satisfied with your design, fix the shells in position on the window box, using a glue gun.

2 Place crocks or pebbles over the drainage holes inside the window box.

3 Partly fill the box with compost, adding water-retaining gel and plant food granules as you go.

4 Place the lavenders at the back of the box. Press extra compost in front of them until it is the right height for the violas. Plant the violas on this "raised bed".

5 Press more compost firmly around all the plants and water generously.

The Planting Projects

Colour Schemes for Containers

The artistry of container gardening lies in the way in which you arrange and combine all your raw materials: not just the plants themselves, but the container and the site you choose for it. Above all, sensitive colour co-ordination can make the difference between a planting scheme that is just pretty and one that draws gasps of admiration. The plants and the container need to enhance each other: lavender with blue violas in a stone urn, for instance, or fiery nasturtiums in terracotta pots. Think about the background, too – the colour of the surrounding walls, the paint on the window frame – and make the picture work as a whole.

Single-colour schemes can be striking, emphasizing the contrasting forms of the flowers and foliage, but so can strong contrasts of colour or tone. Let the glowing palette presented on the following pages inspire you to new heights of creativity.

ABOVE: *Pure white petunias and lobelia planted with a touch of grey foliage make a sophisticated display.*

A Delicate Antique Basket

An antique basket is not essential for this scheme, but the bowl shape makes an interesting variation. A small variety of dahlia, known as a dahlietta, has large white flowers that blend with trailing verbenas and a begonia. Silver-leaved marguerites, with soft pink flowers, add a subtle touch of colour.

VERBENA

DAHLIETTA

ARGYRANTHEMUM

BEGONIA

MATERIALS

36 cm (14 in) hanging basket
Sphagnum moss
Compost
Slow-release plant food granules

PLANTS

White Begonia semperflorens
3 white dahliettas
3 white trailing verbenas
3 marguerites (Argyranthemum
'Flamingo')

1 Line the basket with moss and fill with compost. Mix a teaspoon of slow-release plant food granules into the top of the compost.

2 Plant the begonia in the centre and position and plant the dahliettas around the begonia.

3 Plant a verbena to one side of each of the dahliettas. Plant the marguerites, angling them so they will trail over the edge of the basket. Water well and hang in a sunny position.

GARDENER'S TIP

Regular dead-heading of the flowers will keep the basket in tip-top condition. The slow-release plant food granules will give the flowers a regular supply of nutrients provided the basket is not allowed to dry out.

PLANT IN LATE SPRING OR EARLY SUMMER

An All-white Window Box

A painted wooden window box filled with a white pelargonium, verbenas, marguerites, bacopa, and silver senecio is an ideal combination for a summer wedding celebration in the garden.

MATERIALS

45 cm (18 in) slatted wooden window box
Sphagnum moss
Compost
Slow-release plant food granules

PLANTS

White pelargonium
2 white marguerites (argyranthemums)
2 white trailing verbenas
2 Senecio cineraria *'Silver Dust'*
White bacopa

BACOPA

SENECIO

PELARGONIUM

MARGUERITE

VERBENA

1 It is a good idea to line slatted wooden containers with moss before planting to prevent the compost from leaking out when the box is watered.

2 Fill the moss-lined window box with compost, mixing in 2 teaspoons of slow-release plant food granules. Plant the pelargonium in the centre of the window box towards the back.

3 Plant the marguerites on either side of the pelargonium.

4 Plant the trailing verbenas in the two back corners of the window box.

5 Plant the senecios in the front two corners of the window box to frame the bacopa.

6 Plant the bacopa centrally in the front of the box. Water the arrangement thoroughly and stand in a sunny position.

Gardener's Tip

To prolong the life of wooden containers it is advisable to empty them of compost before winter and store them under cover until spring.

PLANT IN LATE SPRING OR EARLY SUMMER

White Flowers and Painted Terracotta

There are plenty of inexpensive window boxes available, but they do tend to look rather similar. Why not customize a bought window box to give it a touch of individuality? This deep blue painted window box creates an interesting setting for the cool white pelargonium and verbenas.

MATERIALS

45 cm (18 in) terracotta window box painted blue
Crocks or other suitable drainage material
Compost
Slow-release plant food granules

PLANTS

White pelargonium
2 variegated felicias
2 white trailing verbenas

FELICIA

VERBENA

PELARGONIUM

1 Cover the base of the window box with a layer of crocks or similar drainage material.

2 Fill the window box with compost, mixing in 2 teaspoons of slow-release plant food granules. Plant the pelargonium in the centre of the window box.

3 Plant a felicia on either side of the pelargonium at the back of the container. Plant a verbena on either side of the pelargonium at the front of the window box. Water well and stand in a sunny position.

GARDENER'S TIP

White pelargoniums need regular dead-heading to look their best. Old flowerheads discolour and quickly spoil the appearance of the plant.

PLANT IN LATE SPRING OR EARLY SUMMER

Wedding Fuchsias

MATERIALS

Wire basket
Sphagnum moss
Garden twine

PLANTS

3 Fuchsia 'Happy Wedding Day'
3 busy Lizzies (impatiens)
  (optional)
3 white lace-cap hydrangeas
  (optional)

'Happy Wedding Day' is a modern fuchsia which produces very large, round flowers. The lax growth makes it highly suitable for use in a decorative wire basket. As its name suggests, this fuchsia is ideal for a wedding display. Other white-flowered plants can be used to make a really imposing display, and to reinforce the lively impact of the fuchsia's fresh white bells.

FUCHSIA

1 Make a hand-sized pad of sphagnum moss and start to cover the outside of the plastic pot containing the fuchsia.

2 Use a long piece of twine to start tying the moss in place. Leave the ends loose.

3 Continue working around the pot, using small pads of moss.

4 Use the long ends of the piece of twine to secure the moss as you work round the pot.

5 Completely cover the pot with moss. Repeat for the other plants. Group the pots together for a finished display.

GARDENER'S TIP

To ensure that you have a vigorous display with lots of flowers on the wedding day, you will need to stop the plants at least eight weeks before. This involves pinching out the sideshoots and growing tips with your fingers. It will encourage extra bushy growth, and the development of even more flower buds.

PLANT IN SPRING OR SUMMER

A Silver and White Wall Basket

The helichrysum's silvery foliage and cool blue lavender flowers give a delicate colour scheme which would look good against a weathered background.

MATERIALS

30 cm (12 in) wall basket
Sphagnum moss
Compost
Slow-release plant food granules

PLANTS

2 lavenders (Lavandula dentata *var.* candicans)
Osteospermum *'Whirligig'*
2 Helichrysum petiolare

OSTEOSPERMUM

LAVENDER

HELICHRYSUM

GARDENER'S TIP

The lavender used in this project is fairly unusual – if you wish, you can substitute a low-growing variety such as 'Hidcote'.
Keep the helichrysum in check by pinching out its growing tips fairly regularly or it may take over the basket.

PLANT IN SPRING

1 Line the basket with moss and half-fill it with compost.

2 Mix in a half-teaspoon of plant food granules. Plant the lavenders in each corner.

3 Plant the osteospermum in the centre of the basket then add the helichrysums on either side.

4 Angle the plants to encourage them to trail over the side of the basket. Fill with compost. Water the basket and hang.

An Informal Wall Basket

The strong pink of the dahlietta flower is echoed in the leaf colouring of the pink-flowered polygonums in this country-style basket. Silver thymes and white lobelias provide a gentle contrast.

MATERIALS

36 cm (14 in) wall basket
Sphagnum moss
Compost
Slow-release plant food granules

PLANTS

5 white lobelias
3 Polygonum 'Pink Bubbles'
2 thymes (Thymus 'Silver Queen')
1 pink dahlietta (miniature dahlia)

LOBELIA

THYME

POLYGONUM

DAHLIETTA

1 Line the back and the base of the basket with moss, and position three lobelias around the side of the basket near the base.

2 Plant two of the polygonums into the side of the basket above the lobelia. Rest the root-balls on the moss, and gently feed the foliage through the basket.

3 Fill the basket with compost. Mix a half-teaspoon of slow-release plant food granules into the top of the compost. Plant the thymes into the corners of the basket, angling them so that they tumble over the sides.

4 Plant the dahlietta in the middle of the basket and the remaining polygonum in front of the dahlietta. Plant the remaining lobelias. Water well and hang in a sunny position.

GARDENER'S TIP

To prevent the thyme getting leggy, trim off all the flowerheads after flowering – this will help to maintain a dense, well-shaped plant.

PLANT IN SPRING

A Medley of Pinks

DIANTHUS

PETUNIA

PELARGONIUM

In this basket-weave stone planter sugar-pink petunias are planted with ivy-leaved pelargoniums and shaggy-flowered pink dianthus with a deep-red eye. None of these plants requires much depth for its roots and, provided the plants are fed and watered regularly, they will be happy.

MATERIALS

60 cm (24 in) window box
Gravel
Compost
Slow-release plant food granules

PLANTS

2 pink-flowered ivy-leaved
*   pelargoniums*
3 sugar-pink petunias
6 pink dianthus

1 Fill the base of the window box with a layer of washed gravel or similar drainage material.

2 Fill the window box with compost, mixing in 2 teaspoons of plant food granules.

3 Plant the two pelargoniums 10 cm (4 in) from either end of the window box.

4 Plant the petunias, evenly spaced, along the back edge of the window box.

5 Plant four dianthus along the front edge, and the other two on either side of the central petunia.

6 Spread a layer of gravel around the plants; this is decorative and also helps to retain moisture. Water well and stand in a sunny position.

GARDENER'S TIP

Once the summer is over, the petunias and pelargoniums will need to be removed, but the dianthus will overwinter quite happily. Cut off any flower stems and add a fresh layer of gravel.

PLANT IN LATE SPRING OR EARLY SUMMER

A Wall Basket in Shades of Pink

Trailing rose-pink petunias provide the main structure of this wall basket and are combined with two colourful verbenas and white alyssum. On their own, the pale petunia flowers could look somewhat insipid but they are enhanced by the deeper tones of the verbenas.

MATERIALS

36 cm (14 in) wall basket
Sphagnum moss
Compost
Slow-release plant food granules

PLANTS

4 white alyssum
2 cascading rose-pink petunias
2 Verbena 'Pink Parfait' and 'Carousel', or similar

ALYSSUM

VERBENA

PETUNIA

1 Line the back of the basket and half-way up the front with moss. Plant the alyssum into the side of the basket, resting the rootballs on the moss and feeding the foliage through the sides.

2 Fill the basket with compost and mix a half-teaspoon of slow-release plant food granules into the top of the compost. Plant the petunias in each corner.

3 Plant the verbenas one in front of the other, in the middle of the basket. Water thoroughly and hang in a sunny position.

GARDENER'S TIP

If, like these petunias, some of the plants are more developed than others, pinch out the growing tips so that all the plants grow together and one variety will not smother the others.

PLANT IN LATE SPRING OR EARLY SUMMER

'Balcon' Pelargoniums

Traditionally planted to cascade from balconies in many European countries, these lovely pelargoniums are now increasingly and deservedly popular. They are seen at their best when planted alone, as in this basket, where the only variation is of colour.

MATERIALS

40 cm (16 in) hanging basket
Sphagnum moss
Compost
Slow-release plant food granules

PLANTS

5 'Balcon' pelargoniums
('Princess of Balcon' and 'King of Balcon' were used here: the former is now often known as 'Roi des Balcons Lilas', and the latter as 'Hederinum')

1 Fully line the basket with moss. Fill with compost. Mix a teaspoon of slow-release plant food granules into the top layer of the compost.

2 Plant one of the pelargoniums in the centre of the basket.

3 Plant the other four pelargoniums round the edge of the basket, and remove any supporting canes to encourage the plants to tumble over the side. Water well and hang the basket up in a sunny spot.

'BALCON'
PELARGONIUMS

GARDENER'S TIP

Take cuttings from non-flowering stems in the autumn to use in next year's basket. Pelargonium cuttings root easily and the young plants can be kept on a window-sill until spring.

PLANT IN LATE SPRING OR
EARLY SUMMER

Sugar and Spice

The candy-floss colour of the petunias is enriched by combining them with deep crimson ivy-leaved pelargoniums. Slower-growing silver-leaved snapdragons and a variegated pelargonium will add further colour later in the summer.

MATERIALS

36 cm (14 in) hanging basket
Sphagnum moss
Compost
Slow-release plant food granules

PLANTS

3 snapdragons (Antirrhinum 'Avalanche') (optional)
Ivy-leaved Pelargonium 'Blue Beard'
Ivy-leaved Pelargonium 'L'Elégante' (optional)
3 pink petunias

SNAPDRAGON

PELARGONIUMS

PETUNIA

GARDENER'S TIP

It is a good idea to include a number of different plants. This creates a more interesting picture and ensures that if one plant does not thrive, as happened to the snapdragons in this basket, the other plants will still make a good display.

PLANT IN LATE SPRING OR
EARLY SUMMER

1 Line the lower half of the basket with moss. Plant the snapdragons in the side of the basket, resting the rootballs on the moss and guiding the foliage through the side of the basket.

2 Line the remainder of the basket with moss, tucking it carefully around the underplanted snapdragons.

3 Fill the basket with compost, mixing a teaspoon of slow-release plant food granules into the top layer of compost. Plant the Pelargonium 'Blue Beard' at the back of the basket.

4 Plant the Pelargonium 'L'Elégante' at the front of the basket. Plant the petunias around the pelargoniums. Water thoroughly and hang in a sunny position.

Three Tiers of Colour

Scented petunias, delicate white marguerites and starry isotoma make a stunning layered arrangement. Use veined petunias, as they have the strongest scent.

MATERIALS

36 cm (14 in) terracotta window box
Crocks or other suitable drainage material
Compost
Slow-release plant food granules

PLANTS

2 white marguerites (argyranthemums)
3 petunias
3 isotoma

ISOTOMA

MARGUERITE

PETUNIA

GARDENER'S TIP

Try to position flowers where they can be seen at dusk, when their colours become far more intense and are a treat not to be missed.

PLANT IN LATE SPRING OR EARLY SUMMER

1 Cover the base of the window box with crocks. Fill with compost, mixing in 2 teaspoons of slow-release plant food granules.

2 Plant the marguerites on either side of the centre towards the back of the window box.

3 Plant one petunia in the centre and the other two at each end of the window box.

4 Plant the isotoma along the front edge of the window box. Water the arrangement well and stand in a sunny position.

Divine Magenta

The gloriously strong colour of magenta petunias is combined with blue *Convolvulus sabatius*, heliotropes, which will bear scented deep purple flowers, and a variegated scented-leaf pelargonium, which will add colour and fragrance later in the summer.

MATERIALS

45 cm (18in) basket
Sphagnum moss
Compost
Slow-release plant food granules

PLANTS

Scented-leaf Pelargonium
  'Fragrans Variegatum'
3 purple heliotropes
3 Convolvulus sabatius
5 trailing magenta-flowered
  petunias

HELIOTROPES

PELARGONIUM

CONVOLVULUS

PETUNIA

1 Carefully line the hanging basket with a thick layer of moss.

2 Fill the basket with compost, mixing a teaspoon of slow-release plant food granules into the top layer.

3 Plant the scented-leaf pelargonium in the middle of the hanging basket.

4 Plant the heliotropes, evenly spaced, around the central pelargonium.

5 Plant the blue convolvulus, evenly spaced, around the edge of the basket.

6 Plant the petunias in the spaces between the convolvulus and the heliotropes.

GARDENER'S TIP

Baskets with flat bases like this one can be stood on columns rather than hung from brackets. This is a useful solution if fixing a bracket is difficult.

PLANT IN LATE SPRING OR EARLY SUMMER

A Peachy Pink Wall Basket

The vivid flowers of the petunias and pelargonium contrast dramatically with the greeny-yellow lamiums. This basket is seen to best effect against a dark background.

LAMIUM

PETUNIA

PELARGONIUM

MATERIALS

30 cm (12 in) wide wall basket
Sphagnum moss
Compost
Slow-release plant food granules

PLANTS

3 Lamium *'Golden Nuggets'*
Peach/pink *zonal* Pelargonium
 'Palais', or similar
3 petunias

1 Line the back and lower half of the front of the basket with moss. Plant the lamiums by resting the rootballs on the moss, and feeding the foliage through the side of the basket. Line the rest of the basket with moss.

2 Fill the basket with compost, mixing a half-teaspoon of slow-release plant food granules into the top layer. Plant the pelargonium in the centre of the basket against the back edge.

3 Plant one petunia in each corner and the third in front of the pelargonium. Water well and hang on a sunny wall.

GARDENER'S TIP

For a gentler colour scheme, the lamium can be replaced with the silver-grey foliage of *Helichrysum microphyllum*.

PLANT IN LATE SPRING OR EARLY SUMMER

A Small Pelargonium Basket

Ivy-leaved pelargoniums are lovely plants for hanging baskets, and one plant will fill a small basket like this by the middle of summer. The silver-leaved helichrysum and lilac diascias add the finishing touches to this pretty pink-and-silver theme.

MATERIALS

25 cm (10 in) hanging basket
Sphagnum moss
Compost
Slow-release plant food granules

PLANTS

2 Diascia 'Lilac Belle'
Ivy-leaved Pelargonium 'Super Rose'
2 Helichrysum microphyllum

DIASCIA

HELICHRYSUM

PELARGONIUM

GARDENER'S TIP

If you like some height in your hanging basket, use small canes to support some of the pelargonium's stems; if you prefer a cascading effect, leave the pelargonium unsupported.

PLANT IN LATE SPRING OR EARLY SUMMER

1 Line the bottom half of the hanging basket with moss.

2 Plant the diascias into the side of the basket by resting the rootballs on the moss, and gently feeding the foliage between the wires. Add some compost.

3 Line the rest of the basket with moss, top up with compost and mix a teaspoon of slow-release plant food granules into the top layer. Plant the pelargonium in the centre of the basket.

4 Plant the helichrysums on either side of the pelargonium. Water the basket well and hang in a sunny position.

Luxury Basket

Fuchsia 'Pink Galore' is a beautiful cultivar for a luxury hanging basket. The dark glossy green foliage is a perfect foil for the very full, soft rose-pink flowers. A plastic basket with a fixed reservoir has been used to facilitate growth and watering, and the curtain of stems will soon hide the basket from view.

FUCHSIA

MATERIALS

36 cm (14 in) plastic hanging basket with fixed reservoir
Compost
Slow-release plant food granules

PLANTS

5 Fuchsia 'Pink Galore'

1 To avoid the plants becoming tangled in the chain, pull it to one side while planting up the basket.

2 Put a layer of compost with a half-teaspoon of slow-release plant food granules into the bottom of the hanging basket.

3 Arrange four of the plants around the edge of the basket in a symmetrical pattern. Place the last plant centrally.

4 Remove each fuchsia plant from its pot, and gently ease the rootball into the compost.

5 Carefully fill the spaces between the plants with more compost mixed with plant food granules. Firm the compost with your hands.

6 Tease the stems and the foliage around the chains as they are lifted into position.

GARDENER'S TIP

Always use an odd number of plants to achieve the best effect.
A plant placed centrally will prevent a gap appearing as the plants begin to cascade downwards.

PLANT IN EARLY SUMMER

In the Pink

The common name for *Dianthus deltoides* is the pink. Its delightful deeply coloured flowers and silvery grey foliage work very well in a hanging basket combined with prostrate thymes, pink-flowered verbena and an osteospermum.

MATERIALS

36 cm (14 in) hanging basket
Sphagnum moss
Compost
Slow-release plant food granules

PLANTS

6 Dianthus deltoides
Osteospermum *'Pink Whirls'*
Verbena *'Silver Anne'*
3 thymes (Thymus *'Pink Chintz'*
or similar prostrate variety)

PINKS

THYME

VERBENA

OSTEOSPERMUM

GARDENER'S TIP

Pinch out the growing tips regularly to prevent plants such as the osteospermum growing too vigorously upwards and unbalancing the look of the basket. It will be bushier and more in scale with the other plants as a result.

PLANT IN SPRING

1 Line the bottom half of the basket with moss and fill with compost. Plant three of the pinks into the side of the basket, resting the rootballs on the compost and feeding the leaves carefully through the wire.

2 Line the rest of the basket with moss and fill with compost. Mix a teaspoon of slow-release plant food granules into the top of the compost. Plant the osteospermum in the centre of the hanging basket.

3 Plant the verbena to one side of the osteospermum on the edge of the basket and the thymes, evenly spaced, around the unplanted edge.

4 Plant the remaining three pinks between the thymes and the verbena. Water well and hang in a sunny position.

Bright Splashes of Colour

MATERIALS

*76 cm (30 in) plastic window
   box with drainage holes*
Compost
Slow-release plant food granules

PLANTS

2 yellow gazanias
3 Alaska nasturtiums
3 Brachycome 'Lemon Mist'
*2 yellow snapdragons
   (antirrhinums)*

The leaves of the Alaska nasturtium look as if they have been splattered with cream paint. In this box they are planted with yellow-flowered snapdragons, gazanias and brachycome daisies.

BRACHYCOME

NASTURTIUM

SNAPDRAGONS

GAZANIA

GARDENER'S TIP

Nasturtiums are among the easiest
plants to grow from seed.
Start them off about 4–6 weeks
before you plant your window box,
potting them on to keep them
growing vigorously.

PLANT IN THE SPRING

1 Fill the window box with compost, mixing in 2 teaspoons of plant food. Plant the gazanias either side of the centre.

2 Plant the nasturtiums at either end and in the centre of the window box.

3 Plant the three brachycome plants, evenly spaced, along the front of the window box.

4 Plant the two snapdragons on either side of the central nasturtium. Water thoroughly and stand in a sunny position.

Fire and Earth

NASTURTIUM

FUCHSIA

LOTUS

The earth tones of this small decorative terracotta window box are topped with the fiery reds and oranges of the plants – the fuchsia with its orange foliage and tubular scarlet flowers, the orange nasturtiums and the red claw-like flowers of the feathery-leaved lotus.

MATERIALS

36 cm (14 in) terracotta window box
Clay granules or other suitable drainage
  material
Compost
Slow-release plant food granules

PLANTS

Fuchsia 'Thalia'
3 orange nasturtiums
2 Lotus berthelotii

1 Cover the base of the window box with drainage material. Fill with compost, mixing in a teaspoon of plant food granules.

2 Plant the fuchsia in the centre of the window box.

3 Plant the nasturtiums along the back of the window box.

4 Plant the two lotuses in the front of the window box on either side of the fuchsia. Water thoroughly, leave to drain, and stand in a sunny position.

GARDENER'S TIP

This stunning fuchsia is worth keeping for next year.
Pot it up in the autumn, cut back by half and overwinter on a window-sill or in a heated greenhouse.

PLANT IN LATE SPRING OR
EARLY SUMMER

Fruit and Flowers

Bright red petunias become even more vibrant when interplanted with variegated helichrysums and underplanted with alpine strawberries. With their delicate trailing tendrils, the strawberry plants soften the lower edge of the basket.

MATERIALS

30 cm (12 in) hanging basket
Sphagnum moss
Compost
Slow-release plant food granules

PLANTS

3 alpine strawberry plants
3 bright red petunias
3 Helichrysum petiolare
  'Variegatum'

HELICHRYSUM

ALPINE STRAWBERRY

PETUNIA

GARDENER'S TIP

The tendrils, or runners, sent out by the strawberries are searching for somewhere to root. If you can fix a pot in a suitable spot, pin the plantlet into the compost while it is still attached to the parent plant. As soon as it has rooted it can be cut free.

PLANT IN LATE SPRING OR
EARLY SUMMER

1 Line the lower half of the basket with moss.

2 Plant the alpine strawberries by resting the rootballs on the moss, and guiding the leaves through the side of the basket.

3 Line the rest of the basket with moss and fill with compost. Mix in a teaspoon of slow-release plant food granules. Plant the petunias, evenly spaced, in the top of the basket.

4 Interplant the petunias with the helichrysums. Water thoroughly and hang in full or partial shade.

Flame-red Flowers in Terracotta

The intense red flowers of the pelargoniums, verbena and nasturtiums are emphasized by a few yellow nasturtiums and the variegated ivy, but cooled slightly by the soothing blue-green of the nasturtium's umbrella-shaped leaves.

NASTURTIUM

VERBENA

IVY

PELARGONIUM

MATERIALS

50 cm (20 in) terracotta window box
Crocks or other suitable drainage material
Compost
Slow-release plant food granules

PLANTS

2 red zonal pelargoniums
2 nasturtiums – 1 red, 1 yellow
Red verbena
2 variegated ivies

1 Place a layer of crocks or other suitable drainage material in the base of the window box.

2 Fill the container with compost, mixing in 3 teaspoons of slow-release plant food granules.

3 Plant the pelargoniums either side of the centre of the window box.

4 Plant a nasturtium at each end of the window box, in the back corners.

5 Plant the verbena in the centre of the window box.

6 Plant the ivies in front of the nasturtiums in the corners. Water well, leave to drain, and place in a sunny position.

GARDENER'S TIP

Nasturtiums are prone to attack by blackfly. Treat at the first sign of infestation with a suitable insecticide and the plants will remain healthy.

PLANT IN LATE SPRING OR EARLY SUMMER

Sunny Daisies and Violas

Osteospermum daisies are sun-worshippers, keeping their petals furled in cloudy weather. In this window box they are combined with yellow violas and tumbling white bacopas.

VIOLA

BACOPA

OSTEOSPERMUM

MATERIALS

45 cm (18in) fibre window box
Polystyrene or other suitable
  drainage material
Compost
Slow-release plant food granules

PLANTS

Osteospermum 'Buttermilk'
3 yellow violas
2 white bacopas

1 Line the base of the box with polystyrene or other suitable drainage material and fill with compost.

2 Mix in 3 teaspoons of plant food granules. Plant the osteospermum in the centre.

3 Plant two of the violas at each end of the window box and the third in front of the osteospermum.

4 Plant the two bacopas on either side of the osteospermum. Stand in a sunny spot and water thoroughly.

GARDENER'S TIP

Pinch out the growing tips of the osteospermum regularly to encourage a bushy rather than a leggy plant.

PLANT IN SPRING

A Floral Chandelier

MATERIALS

36 cm (14 in) hanging basket
Sphagnum moss
Compost
Slow-release plant food granules

PLANTS

3 yellow lantanas, 2 variegated,
*   1 green-leaved*
2 Bidens ferulifolia
5 African marigolds (tagetes)

The chandelier shape is a result of combining the spreading bidens with upright lantanas and marigolds. Since the variegated-leaf lantanas proved very slow to establish, a more vigorous green-leaved form was added later. As the season progresses, the strongly marked leaves of the variegated plants will become more dominant.

AFRICAN MARIGOLDS

LANTANA

BIDENS

1 Line the basket with moss. Fill it with compost, mixing a teaspoon of slow-release plant food granules into the top layer. Plant the lantana in the centre.

2 Plant the two bidens opposite one another at the edge of the basket.

3 Plant the African marigolds around the lantana plants. Water thoroughly and hang in a sunny position.

GARDENER'S TIP

To complete the chandelier, make candle holders by twisting thick garden wire around the base of yellow candles and add them to the hanging basket.

PLANT IN LATE SPRING OR EARLY SUMMER

Vibrant Reds and Sunny Yellows

This basket is an exciting mix of glowing colours and contrasting leaf shapes. A bright red verbena and the pineapple-scented salvia tumble from the basket, intertwined with red and yellow nasturtiums and a striking golden grass.

NASTURTIUM

VERBENA

SALVIA

GOLDEN GRASS

MATERIALS

36 cm (14 in) hanging basket
Sphagnum moss
Compost
Slow-release plant food granules

PLANTS

4 trailing nasturtiums
Golden grass Hakonechloa
  'Alboaurea', or similar
Salvia elegans
Verbena 'Lawrence Johnston'

1 Line the bottom half of the basket with moss.

2 Plant three of the nasturtiums into the side of the basket by resting the rootballs on the moss, and carefully feeding the leaves through the basket.

3 Line the rest of the basket with moss and fill with compost. Mix a teaspoon of slow-release plant food granules into the compost. Plant the golden grass to one side of the basket.

4 Plant the salvia a third of the way round the edge of the basket from the grass.

5 Plant the verbena at an equal distance from the salvia and the golden grass.

6 Plant the remaining nasturtium in the centre. Water well and hang in a sunny position.

GARDENER'S TIP

Nasturtiums are wonderful plants for hanging baskets – vigorous, colourful and undemanding – but they can be disfigured by blackfly. Spray at the first sign of an infestation with an insecticide which will not harm beneficial insects.

PLANT IN LATE SPRING OR EARLY SUMMER

Summer Carnival

The orange markings on the throats of some of the mimulus flowers look wonderful with the orange-flowered pelargonium in this colourful basket. By the end of the season, trails of lysimachia leaves will form a waterfall of foliage around the base.

MATERIALS

36 cm (14 in) basket
Sphagnum moss
Compost
Slow-release plant food granules

PLANTS

Orange-flowered zonal
* pelargonium*
3 Lysimachia nummularia 'Aurea'
3 mimulus

LYSIMACHIA

MIMULUS

PELARGONIUM

GARDENER'S TIP

Dead-head the flowers regularly to encourage repeat flowering, and if the mimulus start to get leggy, cut back the offending stems to a leaf joint. New shoots will soon appear.

PLANT IN LATE SPRING OR EARLY SUMMER

1 Line the basket with moss and fill it with compost, mixing a teaspoon of slow-release plant food granules into the top layer. Plant the pelargonium in the centre of the basket.

2 Plant the lysimachia, evenly spaced, around the edge of the basket, angling the plants so they will trail over the sides.

3 Plant the mimulus between the lysimachia. Water the hanging basket thoroughly and hang in a sunny spot.

Tumbling Violas

Violas can be surprisingly vigorous plants and, given the space, will happily tumble over the edge of a wall basket. Combined with curly-leaved parsley and the daisy-like flowers of asteriscus the effect is delicate but luxuriant.

MATERIALS

30 cm (12 in) wall basket
Compost
Sphagnum moss
Slow-release plant food granules

PLANTS

5 parsley plants
5 yellow violas
Asteriscus 'Gold Coin'

PARSLEY

ASTERISCUS

VIOLA

1 Line the back and lower half of the front of the basket with sphagnum moss.

2 Plant three of the parsley plants into the sides of the basket by resting the rootballs on the moss, and feeding the foliage through the wires.

3 Add another layer of moss and plant two of the viola plants in the side of the basket using the same method.

4 Finish lining the basket with moss and fill with compost, mixing a half-teaspoon of slow-release plant food granules into the top layer. Plant the asteriscus in the centre of the basket, and surround with the remaining parsley and viola plants.

GARDENER'S TIP

To keep the violas flowering all summer they need regular dead-heading – the easiest way to do this is to give the plants a trim with a pair of scissors rather than trying to remove heads individually.

PLANT IN SPRING

Mediterranean Mood

The lantana is a large shrub which thrives in a Mediterranean or sub-tropical climate, but it is increasingly popular in cooler climates as a half-hardy perennial in borders and containers. This multi-coloured variety has been planted with yellow bidens and orange dahliettas.

MATERIALS

36 cm (14 in) hanging basket
Sphagnum moss
Compost
Slow-release plant food granules

PLANTS

Orange/pink lantana
3 orange dahliettas (miniature dahlias)
3 Bidens aurea

DAHLIETTA

BIDENS

LANTANA

1 Line the basket with moss. Fill the basket with compost, mixing a teaspoon of slow-release plant food granules into the top layer. Plant the lantana in the centre of the basket.

2 Plant the dahliettas, evenly spaced, around the lantana.

3 Plant the bidens between the dahliettas. Water thoroughly and hang in a sunny position.

GARDENER'S TIP

To encourage a bushy plant, pinch out the growing tips of the lantana regularly. Like many popular plants, the lantana is poisonous, so treat it with respect and do not try eating it.

PLANT IN LATE SPRING OR EARLY SUMMER

A Sunny Wall Basket

MATERIALS

30 cm (12 in) wall basket
Sphagnum moss
Compost
Slow-release plant food granules

PLANTS

2 Lysimachia congestiflora
3 Alaska nasturtiums
3 mixed colour African marigolds
(tagetes)

LYSIMACHIA

NASTURTIUM

AFRICAN
MARIGOLDS

The vibrant yellows, oranges and reds of the flowers in this basket glow richly amongst the variegated leaves of the nasturtiums. As the season progresses the underplanted lysimachia will bear deep yellow flowers and add another layer of colour.

1 Line the back of the basket and half-way up the front with moss. Plant the lysimachia by resting the rootballs on the moss and feeding the foliage between the wires.

2 Line the rest of the basket and fill with compost, mixing in a half-teaspoon of plant food granules. Plant the nasturtiums along the back.

3 Plant the African marigolds in front of the nasturtiums. Water the basket well and hang it up in a sunny spot.

GARDENER'S TIP

If you have a large area of wall to cover, group two or three wall baskets together. This looks very effective, especially when they are planted with the same plants.

PLANT IN SPRING

Dark Drama

The intense purple of the heliotrope usually dominates other plants, but here it is teamed with a selection of equally dramatic colours – *Dahlia* 'Bednall Beauty', with its purple foliage and dark red flowers, black grass and red and purple verbenas – to make a stunning display.

MATERIALS

60 cm (24 in) terracotta window box
Broken polystyrene or other suitable drainage material
Compost
Slow-release plant food granules

PLANTS

Heliotrope
2 Dahlia 'Bednall Beauty'
Black grass (Ophiopogon planiscapus 'Nigrescens')
2 purple trailing verbenas
2 red trailing verbenas

BLACK GRASS

VERBENAS

DAHLIA

HELIOTROPE

1 Fill the bottom of the window box with broken polystyrene or other suitable drainage material.

2 Fill the window box with compost, mixing in 3 teaspoons of slow-release plant food granules. Plant the heliotrope centrally at the back of the window box, gently teasing apart the roots, if necessary.

3 Plant the dahlias in the back corners of the window box.

4 Plant the black grass in front of the heliotrope.

5 Plant the purple verbenas at the back between the heliotrope and the dahlias.

6 Plant the red verbenas at the front in either corner. This is a large container so it is best to position it before watering. Put it where it will benefit from full sun, then water thoroughly.

GARDENER'S TIP

Dahlias can be overwintered by digging up the tubers after the first frosts, cutting the stems back to 15 cm (6 in) and drying them off before storing in slightly damp peat in a frost-free shed. Start into growth again in spring and plant out after all danger of frost is past.

PLANT IN LATE SPRING OR EARLY SUMMER

A Cascade of Lilac and Silver

Lilac petunias and violas are surrounded by a cascading curtain of variegated ground ivy and silver-leaved senecio in this softly coloured hanging basket.

MATERIALS

30 cm (12 in) hanging basket
Sphagnum moss
Compost
Slow-release plant food granules

PLANTS

3 deep blue violas
3 soft blue petunias
*Variegated ground ivy (Glechoma
  hederacea 'Variegata')*
3 Senecio cineraria 'Silver Dust'

SENECIO

IVY

PETUNIA

VIOLAS

GARDENER'S TIP

If the ground ivy becomes too rampant and threatens to throttle the other plants, prune it by removing some of the stems completely and reducing the length of the others.

PLANT IN LATE SPRING OR EARLY SUMMER

1 Line the lower half of the basket with moss. Plant the violas in the side by resting the rootballs on the moss, and carefully guiding the foliage between the wires. Line the rest of the basket with moss and fill with compost, mixing a teaspoon of slow-release plant food granules into the top layer.

2 Plant the three petunias, evenly spaced, in the top of the basket. Plant the ground ivy on one side to trail over the edge of the basket.

3 Plant the three senecios between the petunias. Water well and hang in a sunny position.

Violas and Verbenas

Deep blue violas are surrounded by trailing
purple verbenas to make a simple but attractive
basket. Trailing verbena is a particularly good
hanging-basket plant with its feathery foliage
and pretty flowers.

VERBENA

VIOLAS

MATERIALS

30 cm (12 in) hanging basket
Sphagnum moss
Compost
Slow-release plant food granules

PLANTS

9 blue violas
3 purple trailing verbenas

1 Line the lower half of the
basket with moss. Plant five of
the violas into the side of the
basket by resting the rootballs on
the moss and guiding the foliage
through the side of the basket.

2 Line the rest of the basket with
moss and fill with compost,
mixing a teaspoon of slow-release
plant food granules into the top
layer. Plant the verbenas around
the edge of the basket.

3 Plant the remaining violas in
the centre of the basket. Water
well and hang in partial sun.

GARDENER'S TIP

If the violas grow too tall, pinch out
the main stems of the plants to
encourage the spreading side shoots.

PLANT IN SPRING

An Instant Garden

There is not always time to wait for a window box to grow and this is one solution. Fill a container with potted plants and, as the season progresses, you can ring the changes by removing those that are past their best and introducing new plants.

HELICHRYSUM

PETUNIA

MATERIALS

64 cm (25 in) galvanized tin
  window box
Clay granules
5 1-litre (5 in) plastic pots
Compost

PLANTS

Lavender (Lavandula pinnata)
2 blue petunias
Convolvulus sabatius
Blue bacopa
Helichrysum petiolare
Viola 'Jupiter'

LAVENDER

CONVOLVULUS

GARDENER'S TIP

When using a container without drainage holes, take care not to
overwater or the roots will become waterlogged.
Check after heavy rain, too, and empty away any excess water.

VIOLA

BACOPA

PLANT IN LATE SPRING OR EARLY SUMMER

1 Fill the base of the container with clay granules or similar drainage material.

2 Pot up the lavender into one of the pots.

3 Pot up one of the petunias with the convolvulus.

4 Pot up the other petunia with the bacopa.

5 Pot up the helichrysum.

6 Pot up the viola and arrange the pots in the window box.

Showers of Flowers

Deep, velvety purple pansies and purple sage are surrounded by pink nemesias and tumbling purple verbenas in a pretty basket hung, here, in the corner of a thatched summerhouse.

MATERIALS

40 cm (16 in) hanging basket
Sphagnum moss
Compost
Slow-release plant food granules

PLANTS

3 purple verbenas
Purple sage
3 deep purple pansies
6 Nemesia 'Confetti'

VERBENA

SAGE

PANSY

NEMESIA

GARDENER'S TIP

In summer, pansies tend to flag in hot sun, especially in hanging baskets. They will do best where they are in the shade during the hottest part of the day.

PLANT IN SPRING

1 Line the lower half of the basket with moss. Plant the verbenas in the side of the basket. Line the rest of the basket and fill with compost, mixing in a teaspoon of plant food granules.

2 Plant the sage in the middle of the basket.

3 Plant the three purple pansies around the sage, spacing them evenly. Add more compost around the pansies and press in firmly.

4 Plant three nemesias at the back of the pansies, and three nemesias between the pansies. Water and hang in light shade.

A Pretty Stencilled Planter

This small stencilled wooden window box is full of blue flowers. In a particularly pretty mix, petunias are intertwined with brachycome daisies and trailing convolvulus. A pair of brackets hold it in place under the window.

MATERIALS

40 cm (16 in) wooden window box
Clay granules or other suitable drainage material
Compost
Slow-release plant food granules

PLANTS

3 blue petunias
2 blue brachycome daisies
Convolvulus sabatius

BRACHYCOME

PETUNIA

CONVOLVULUS

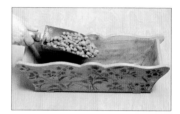

1 Line the base of the window box with clay granules or other suitable drainage material. Fill the window box with compost, mixing in a teaspoon of slow-release plant food granules.

2 Plant the three petunias, evenly spaced, towards the back of the box. Plant the brachycome daisies between the petunias.

3 Plant the convolvulus centrally at the front of the box. Water thoroughly and position in full or partial sun.

GARDENER'S TIP

If you are stencilling a wooden container for outside use, do not forget to seal the wood after decorating it. In this instance, a matt wood varnish in a light oak tint has been used.

PLANT IN LATE SPRING OR EARLY SUMMER

Marguerites and Pimpernels

We are more familiar with the wild scarlet pimpernel, but in this window box its blue relative, anagallis, has been planted to climb among the stems of the yellow marguerites and snapdragons. Blue-flowered variegated felicia and golden helichrysum complete the picture.

MATERIALS

76 cm (30 in) plastic window box
Compost
Slow-release plant food granules

PLANTS

2 yellow marguerites
4 blue anagallis
3 variegated felicias
2 Helichrysum petiolare 'Aureum'
4 yellow snapdragons (Antirrhinum)

MARGUERITE

ANAGALLIS

HELICHRYSUM

SNAPDRAGONS

FELICIA

1 Check the drainage holes are open in the base and, if not, drill or punch them open. Fill the window box with compost, mixing in 3 teaspoons of slow-release plant food granules.

2 Plant the marguerites on either side of the centre, towards the middle of the window box.

3 Plant two of the anagallis in the back corners of the window box and two at the front, on either side of the marguerites.

4 Plant one felicia in the centre of the box and the other two on either side of the anagallis.

5 Plant the helichrysum in the front corners of the window box to trail over the edges.

6 Plant two of the snapdragons on either side of the central felicia and two on either side of the marguerites. Water thoroughly, drain, and stand in a sunny or partially sunny position.

GARDENER'S TIP

Dead-head the marguerites, snapdragons and felicias to keep them flowering all summer. When planting the marguerites, pinch out the growing tips to encourage bushy plants.

PLANT IN SPRING

Shades of Mauve

AGERATUM

ISOTOMA

HELICHRYSUM

SCABIOUS

MATERIALS

40 cm (16 in) hanging basket
Sphagnum moss
Compost
Slow-release plant food granules

PLANTS

6 blue ageratum
Blue scabious
3 Helichrysum petiolare
3 blue Isotoma axillaris

Some unlikely plants, such as this powder-blue scabious, can do very well in a hanging basket, especially when combined, as it is here, with isotoma and ageratum in the same colour, and the trailing silver foliage of helichrysum.

1 Line the lower half of the basket with moss. Plant three ageratum by resting the rootballs on the moss, and carefully guiding the foliage through the wires.

2 Add a further layer of moss and plant the other three ageratum into the side of the basket at a higher level.

3 Fill the basket with compost, mixing a teaspoon of slow-release plant food granules into the top layer. Plant the scabious in the centre of the basket.

4 Plant the helichrysums, evenly spaced, around the edge of the basket. Plant the isotoma between the helichrysums. Water well and hang in a sunny position.

GARDENER'S TIP

At the end of the season the scabious can be removed from the basket and planted in the border to flower for many years to come.

PLANT IN LATE SPRING

Sapphires for Spring

Deep blue pansies are surrounded by gentian-blue anagallis and underplanted with golden helichrysums in this richly coloured basket.

MATERIALS

30 cm (12 in) hanging basket
Sphagnum moss
Compost
Slow-release plant food granules

PLANTS

3 Helichrysum petiolare 'Aureum'
3 deep blue pansies
3 blue anagallis

ANAGALLIS

HELICHRYSUM

PANSY

1 Line the lower half of the basket with moss before planting the helichrysums in the sides of the basket.

2 Rest the rootballs on the moss, and carefully guide the foliage through the wires.

3 Line the rest of the basket with moss and fill with compost, mixing a teaspoon of plant food into the top layer. Plant the pansies, evenly spaced, in the top of the basket.

4 Plant the anagallis between the pansies. Water the basket thoroughly and hang in partial sun.

GARDENER'S TIP

The golden-green colour of
Helichrysum petiolare 'Aureum'
is far stronger if the
plants are not in full sun.
Too much sun tends to fade
the colouring.

PLANT IN SPRING

Seasonal Planters

There's no need to confine your ideas to summer planting schemes, however
exuberant. You can keep boxes and hanging baskets looking vibrant and beautiful all
year round. It's a lovely reassurance that spring is on its way to see the earliest
spring bulbs bursting into flower right outside your window, and judiciously planted pots
can often be slipped into temporary gaps in the borders to bridge the seasons.
One of the joys of container gardening is that you can put together combinations that
will look their best in spring, summer or autumn, then swap them around to take
centre stage at the appropriate time.

You may also have containers you don't want to move: if a stately classical urn is a
focal point in your garden, give it all-year-round interest with an evergreen shrub
or a beautifully clipped piece of topiary; you can ring seasonal changes by underplanting
with spring and summer bedding plants.

ABOVE: A colourful spring display underplanted with moss.

Daffodils and Wallflowers

A weathered wooden tub planted in the autumn with daffodil bulbs and wallflower plants will provide a colourful spring display. Alternatively, you can buy pots of daffodils and wallflowers in bud in the early spring and plant them for an instant show.

MATERIALS

36 cm (14 in) wooden tub
Polystyrene or other drainage
  material
Compost
Slow-release plant food granules

PLANTS

24 daffodil bulbs or 4 1-litre
  (5 in) pots of daffodils
3 bushy wallflower (cheiranthus)
  plants

1 Break the polystyrene into large pieces and fill the bottom third of the tub to provide drainage and to save on the quantity of compost used.

2 Add compost until the tub is half-full and arrange 12 of the daffodil bulbs evenly over the surface. Cover the bulbs with compost.

3 Arrange the remaining 12 bulbs on the surface of the compost. Remove the wallflower plants from their pots and place them on the compost. Don't worry if the plants cover some of the bulbs, they will grow round the wallflowers. Fill the tub with compost, pressing down firmly around the wallflowers to ensure that they do not work loose in windy weather. Sprinkle a tablespoon of plant food granules on to the surface and work into the top layer of compost.

DAFFODIL

WALLFLOWER

GARDENER'S TIP

To save the bulbs for next year, allow the leaves to die right back and then dig up and store in a cool dry place.

PLANT BULBS IN THE
AUTUMN OR PLANTS IN BUD
IN SPRING

Miniature Spring Garden

Terracotta pots filled with crocuses, irises and primroses nestling in a bed of moss, make a delightful scaled-down spring garden which would fit on the smallest balcony or even a window-sill.

IRIS

MOSS

CROCUS

PRIMROSE

MATERIALS

Terracotta seed tray
2 terracotta pots, 13 cm (5 in) high
Crocks
Compost
Bun moss

PLANTS

3 primroses
Pot of Iris reticulata
Pot of crocuses

1 Cover the drainage holes of the seed tray and the two pots with crocks.

2 Half-fill the seed tray with compost. Before planting the primroses, loosen the roots by gently squeezing the rootball and teasing the roots loose.

3 Arrange the primroses in the seed tray and fill in with compost around the plants, pressing down around the plants to ensure they are firmly planted.

4 Arrange the bun moss around the plants so that all the compost is hidden.

5 Remove the irises from their plastic pot and slip them into a terracotta pot. Bed them in with a little extra compost if necessary, and then arrange moss around the base of the stems.

6 Repeat this process with the crocuses and then water all the containers and arrange them together.

GARDENER'S TIP

Once the irises and crocuses are past their best, hide them behind other pots to die down and dry out before starting them into growth again in the autumn.

PLANT IN EARLY SPRING

Spring Flowers in an Instant

An arrangement of pots of spring flowers is surrounded with bark to give the appearance of a planted window box. As soon as the flowers are over, the pots can be removed and left to die back, and the container is ready for its summer planting.

MATERIALS

40 cm (16 in) terracotta window box
Bark chippings

PLANTS

Pot of daffodils
Pot of yellow tulips
4 yellow pansies in pots

DAFFODIL

PANSY

TULIP

GARDENER'S TIP

Once the flowers have finished and the pots have been removed from the window box, the pots of bulbs can be tucked away in a corner of the garden ready to flower again next year.

PLANT IN LATE WINTER OR EARLY SPRING

1 Position the pot of daffodils at the right-hand end of the window box.

2 Position the pot of tulips at the left-hand end of the window box.

3 Fill the centre and around the pots with bark chippings until the window box is half-full.

4 Position the pansies between the tulips and the daffodils, and add bark until all the pots are concealed. Water moderately and stand in any position.

A Spring Display of Auriculas

An old strawberry punnet carrier makes an attractive and unusual window box in which to display some beautifully marked auriculas planted in antique terracotta pots. A large flower basket or wooden trug would look just as good as this marvellous old wooden carrier.

MATERIALS

8 8–10 cm (3–4 in) old or antique-style terracotta pots
Crocks or other suitable drainage material
Compost
50 cm (20 in) wooden carrier

PLANTS

8 different auriculas (Primula auricula)

AURICULAS

GARDENER'S TIP

A window-sill is an ideal position to see auriculas at their best. It is difficult to admire the full drama of their markings if they are at ground level. When they have finished flowering, stand the pots in a shady corner or a cold frame.

PLANT IN EARLY SPRING

1 Place a crock over the drainage hole of a pot.

2 Remove an auricula from its plastic pot and plant it firmly with added compost.

3 Stand the newly planted auricula in the wooden carrier.

4 Repeat the process for the other plants to fill the carrier. Water thoroughly and stand in light shade.

Display in a Copper Tub

A battered old washing boiler makes an attractive and characterful container for a display of white tulips, underplanted with purple violets and evergreen periwinkles.

MATERIALS

60 cm (24 in) copper boiler
20 cm (8 in) plastic pot
Compost

PLANTS

20 white tulip bulbs
* or tulips in bud*
5 purple violets
2 periwinkles
* (Vinca minor)*

VIOLET

TULIP

PERIWINKLE

GARDENER'S TIP

Lift the tulips when they have finished flowering and hang them up to dry in a cool airy place. They can be replanted late in autumn to flower again next year. Provided you pick off the dead heads, the violets will flower all summer. For a summer display, lift the central violet and plant a standard white marguerite in the centre of the container.

PLANT BULBS IN AUTUMN OR PLANTS IN BUD IN SPRING. PLANT THE VIOLETS AND PERIWINKLES IN SPRING

1 Place the upturned plastic pot in the base of the tub before filling it with compost. This will save on the amount of compost used, and will not have any effect on the growth of the plants as they will still have plenty of room for their roots.

3 Do the underplanting in the early spring. The compost will have settled in the container and should be topped up to within 7.5 cm (3 in) of the rim. Remove the violets from their pots. Gently tweak the rootballs and loosen the roots to aid the plants' growth.

5 Plant a periwinkle on either side of the central violet, again loosening the rootballs.

2 If you are planting tulip bulbs, half-fill the container with compost, arrange the bulbs evenly over the surface and then cover them with a good 15 cm (6 in) of compost. This should be done in late autumn.

4 Plant one violet in the centre and four around the edges. Scoop out the soil by hand to avoid damaging the growing tips of the tulips beneath the surface.

6 If you are planting tulips in bud, the whole scheme should be planted at the same time, interplanting the tulips with the violets and periwinkles. Position in sun or partial shade.

Scented Spring Planter

Lilies-of-the-valley grow very well in containers and they will thrive in the shade where their delicate scented flowers stand out amongst the greenery. Surrounding the plants with bun moss is practical as well as attractive as it will stop the soil splashing back on to the leaves and flowers during fierce spring showers.

MATERIALS

Tinware planter
Clay granules
Compost
Bun moss

PLANTS

6–8 pots of
lily-of-the-
vall.ey

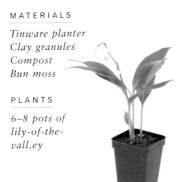

LILY OF THE
VALLEY

1 Fill the bottom of the planter with 5 cm (2 in) of clay granules to improve drainage.

2 Cover the granules with a layer of compost and arrange the lily-of-the-valley plants evenly on the compost.

3 Fill in around the plants with more compost, making sure to press firmly around the plants so that they won't rock about in the wind. Now cover the compost with bun moss, fitting it snugly around the stems of the lily-of-the-valley, as this will also help keep the plants upright.

GARDENER'S TIP

If you want to bring your planter indoors to enjoy the scent of the flowers, use a container without drainage holes in the base, but be very careful not to overwater. Once the plants have finished flowering replant them in a pot with normal drainage holes or in the garden. They are woodland plants and will be quite happy under trees.

PLANT IN EARLY SPRING

Woodland Garden

You do not need your own woodland area for this garden, just a shady corner and an attractive container to hold a selection of plants that thrive in damp shade. The plants are buried in bark chippings in their pots and will relish these conditions as they closely imitate their natural habitat.

MATERIALS

50 cm (20 in) glazed pot
Bark chippings

BLUEBELL

ANEMONE
BLANDA

FERNS

PLANTS

Pot of bluebells
3 hardy ferns
Pot of Anemone blanda

1 Fill the container three-quarters full with bark chippings. Plant your largest pot (in this case the bluebells) first. Scoop a hollow in the bark and position the pot so that the base of the leaves is approximately 5 cm (2 in) below the rim of the container.

2 Cover the pot with bark so that the plastic is no longer visible and the plant is surrounded by chippings.

3 Arrange the ferns so that they relate attractively to one another. Fill the spaces between the ferns with bark.

4 Add the *Anemone blanda* at the front of the container where its flowers will be seen to best advantage, and then top up the whole arrangement with bark. Stand the container in light shade and water.

GARDENER'S TIP

After the bluebells and anemones have finished flowering, lift them out of the container in their pots and set them aside in a shady corner to rest. They can be replaced by other woodland plants such as wild strawberries or periwinkle.

PLANT IN EARLY SPRING

A Garland of Spring Flowers

Miniature daffodils, deep blue pansies, yellow polyanthus and variegated ivy are planted together to make a hanging basket that will flower for many weeks in early spring, lifting the spirits with its fresh colours and delicate woodland charm.

MATERIALS

30 cm (12 in) hanging basket
Sphagnum moss
Compost
Slow-release plant food granules

PLANTS

3 variegated ivies
5 miniature daffodil bulbs 'Tête-à-Tête' or similar, or a pot of daffodils in bud
3 blue pansies
2 yellow polyanthus

POLYANTHUS

IVY

PANSY

MINIATURE DAFFODIL

1 Line the lower half of the basket with moss.

2 Plant the ivies into the side of the basket by resting the rootballs on the moss, and guiding the foliage through the basket so that it will trail down.

3 Line the rest of the basket with moss and add a layer of compost to the bottom of the basket. Push the daffodil bulbs into the compost.

4 Fill the remainder of the basket with compost, mixing a teaspoon of slow-release plant food granules into the top layer. Plant the pansies, evenly spaced, in the top of the basket.

5 Plant the polyanthus between the pansies. Water the basket and hang in sun or shade. If planting daffodils in bud, remove them from the pot and place in the centre of the basket before arranging the ivies and filling with compost.

GARDENER'S TIP

When dismantling the arrangement, plant the variegated ivies in the garden. They look particularly good tumbling over walls, or threading their way through and linking established shrubs. Prune hard if they get out of hand and become too invasive.

PLANT IN AUTUMN IF GROWING DAFFODILS FROM BULBS; IN LATE WINTER OR EARLY SPRING FOR READY-GROWN DAFFODILS

A Basket of Contrasts

The deep green and burgundy foliage of *Fuchsia* 'Thalia' will be even more startling later in summer when the bright red pendant flowers stand out against the leaves and compete with the glowing colours of the nemesias. The yellow-green helichrysums provide a cooling contrast.

MATERIALS

30 cm (12 in) wall basket
Sphagnum moss
Compost
Slow-release plant food granules

PLANTS

3 Helichrysum petiolare
  'Aureum'
Fuchsia 'Thalia'
4 nemesias in red, yellow and
  orange tones

NEMESIA

HELICHRYSUM

FUCHSIA

GARDENER'S TIP

Dead-head the nemesias regularly to ensure that they continue flowering throughout the summer.

PLANT IN LATE SPRING OR
EARLY SUMMER

1 Line the back of the basket and the lower half of the front with moss. Fill the lower half of the basket with compost.

2 Plant two of the helichrysum plants into the side of the basket by resting the rootballs on the moss, and carefully feeding the foliage through the wires.

3 Line the rest of the basket with moss and top up with compost. Mix a half-teaspoon of slow-release plant food granules into the top layer of compost. Plant the fuchsia in the centre.

4 Plant the remaining helichrysum in front of the fuchsia. Plant two nemesias on each side of the central plants. Water the basket well and hang in full or partial sun.

Delicate Summer Flowers

Pale orange pansies contrast beautifully with the lavender-blue convolvulus, and the pastel yellow brachycome daisies link the whole scheme together.

CONVOLVULUS

BRACHYCOME

PANSIES

MATERIALS

30 cm (12 in) hanging basket
Sphagnum moss
Compost
Slow-release plant food granules

PLANTS

3 orange pansies
3 Brachycome *'Lemon Mist'*
2 Convolvulus sabatius

1 Line the basket with moss and fill with compost, mixing a teaspoon of slow-release plant food granules into the top layer. Plant the pansies around the edge.

2 Plant the brachycome daisies between the pansies.

3 Place the convolvulus plants in the centre of the basket so that the tendrils can weave between the other plants. Water and hang in full or partial sun.

GARDENER'S TIP

Each time you water this basket be sure to remove any pansy flowers that are past their best. Once pansies start to set seed they quickly grow leggy and stop flowering.

PLANT IN SPRING

A Mass of Sweet Peas

This large basket is filled with sweet peas surrounding a regal pelargonium. It is inter-planted with chives to provide a contrasting leaf shape and help deter pests. Their fluffy purple flowers will add a further dimension to the arrangement, and the leaves can be snipped off for use in the kitchen.

MATERIALS

40 cm (16 in) hanging basket
Sphagnum moss
Compost
Slow-release plant food granules

PLANTS

Regal Pelargonium 'Sancho Panza'
2–3 small pots or a strip of low-growing sweet peas such as 'Snoopea'
3 chive plants

SWEET PEAS

CHIVES

PELARGONIUM

1 Line the basket with a generous layer of moss.

2 Fill the basket with compost and mix a teaspoon of slow-release plant food granules into the top layer. Plant the regal pelargonium in the centre of the basket.

3 Gently divide the sweet peas into clumps of about eight plants each.

4 Plant the sweet pea clumps around the edge of the basket.

5 Plant the chives between the sweet peas and the central pelargonium.

6 Fill any gaps with more moss. Water well and hang the basket in a sunny position.

GARDENER'S TIP

Sweet peas will bloom longer if you keep picking the flowers and be sure to remove any seed pods as they form. Similarly, the chives grow longer and are stronger if their flowerheads are removed before they seed.

PLANT IN LATE SPRING

Hot Flowers in a Cool Container

Shocking-pink petunias and verbenas are the dominant plants in this window box which also features a softer pink marguerite and silver helichrysum. The dark green of the wooden window box is a pleasing foil for the vibrant flowers.

MATERIALS

76 cm (30 in) plastic window box with drainage holes
90 cm (3 ft) wooden window box (optional)
Compost
Slow-release plant food granules

PLANTS

Trailing pink marguerite (Argyranthemum 'Flamingo')
2 bright pink verbenas, such as 'Sissinghurst'
3 shocking-pink petunias
4 Helichrysum petiolare microphyllum

MARGUERITE

VERBENA

PETUNIA

HELICHRYSUM

GARDENER'S TIP

To add height to this scheme, buy some 30 cm (12 in) green plant sticks. Push two into the soil behind each of the verbenas, and train them upwards.

PLANT IN LATE SPRING OR EARLY SUMMER

1 Fill the plastic window box with compost, mixing in 3 teaspoons of slow-release plant food granules. Plant the marguerite centre front.

2 Plant the verbenas in the back corners of the window box.

3 Plant one of the petunias behind the marguerite, and the other two on either side of it.

4 Plant one helichrysum on each side of the central petunia, and the other two in the front corners of the window box. Water well and lift into place. Stand in a sunny position.

A Lime-green and Blue Box

MATERIALS

76 cm (30 in) plastic window
box with drainage holes
Compost
Slow-release plant food granules

PLANTS

5 lime-green tobacco plants
2 scaevola
2 Helichrysum petiolare 'Aureum'
3 Convolvulus sabatius

Lime-green flowering tobacco and helichrysums contrast
beautifully with the blue scaevolas and convolvulus in this
window box of cool colours.

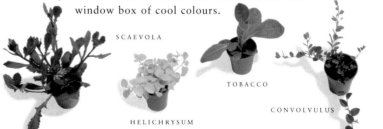

SCAEVOLA

HELICHRYSUM

TOBACCO

CONVOLVULUS

1 Fill the window box with
compost, mixing in 3
teaspoons of plant food granules.
Plant the tobacco plants along the
back of the window box.

2 Plant the two scaevolas
approximately 10 cm (4 in)
from each end, in front of the
tobacco plants.

3 Plant the two helichrysums on
either side of the centre of the
window box next to the scaevolas.

4 Plant two of the convolvulus
in the front corners of the box
and the third in the centre front.
Water thoroughly and position in
light shade or partial sun.

GARDENER'S TIP

At the end of the season pot up the
scaevolas and convolvulus. Cut
right back and protect from frost.

PLANT IN LATE SPRING

A Miniature Cottage Garden

This basket derives its charm from its simple planting scheme. Pot marigolds and parsley are planted with bright blue felicias to create a basket which would look at home on the wall of a cottage or outside the kitchen door.

PARSLEY

FELICIA

POT
MARIGOLDS

MATERIALS

36 cm (14 in) hanging basket
Sphagnum moss
Compost
Slow-release plant food granules

PLANTS

5 parsley plants
3 pot marigolds (Calendula 'Gitana', or similar)
3 felicias

1 Line the lower half of the basket with moss.

2 Plant the parsley into the sides of the basket by resting the rootballs on the moss, and gently feeding the foliage through the wires.

3 Line the rest of the basket with moss, carefully tucking it around the roots of the parsley.

4 Fill the basket with compost, mixing a teaspoon of slow-release plant food granules into the top layer.

5 Plant the three pot marigolds, evenly spaced, in the top of the basket.

6 Plant the felicias between the marigolds. Water well and hang in full or partial sun.

GARDENER'S TIP

Regular dead-heading will keep the basket looking good, but allow at least one of the marigold flowers to form a seedhead and you will be able to grow your own plants next year.

PLANT IN SPRING

Foliage Basket

An old basket makes an ideal container for this interesting group of foliage plants. The different leaf shapes and colours are emphasized when they are grouped together. Including flowers would detract from the architectural quality of the plants.

MATERIALS

30 cm (12 in) basket
Sphagnum moss
Loam-based compost
Slow-release plant food granules
Bark chippings

PLANTS

Phormium tenax
Mexican orange blossom
(Choisya ternata)
Carex brunnea 'Variegata'

CAREX

PHORMIUM

MEXICAN
ORANGE BLOSSOM

GARDENER'S TIP

A planted basket makes an ideal gift for a friend, especially when you have chosen the plants yourself. Include a label, giving the names of the plants and how to care for them.

PLANT AT ANY TIME OF THE YEAR

1 Line the basket with moss. Place the phormium at the back and position the orange blossom next to it.

2 Add the carex and fill between the plants with compost enriched with a tablespoon of slow-release plant food granules.

3 Mulch around the plants with bark chippings. Water well and place in partial shade.

Layers of Flowers

LOBELIAS

TOBACCO

PELARGONIUM

BUSY LIZZIE

MATERIALS

36 cm (14 in) fibre window box
Drainage material
Compost
Slow-release plant food granules

PLANTS

2 white tobacco plants
Variegated Pelargonium
  'l'Elégante'
2 pink busy Lizzies (impatiens)
3 white lobelias

This window box is unusual as the colours are in distinct layers, with upright white flowering tobacco above pink busy Lizzies, and tumbling white variegated pelargonium and lobelias. The fibre window box is concealed by a decorative twig container.

1 Put some drainage material in the base of the window box; fill with compost, mixing in 2 teaspoons of plant food granules. Plant the flowering tobacco near the back edge.

2 Plant the pelargonium at the front of the window box, in the centre.

3 Plant the busy Lizzies at each end of the window box.

4 Plant one of the lobelias between the flowering tobacco, and the other two on either side of the pelargonium.

GARDENER'S TIP

Somehow, rogue blue lobelias have appeared among the white plants. This sort of thing often happens in gardening and, as in this case, the accidental addition can turn out well.

PLANT IN SPRING

Full of Cheer

Vivid red pelargoniums and verbenas are combined with cheerful yellow bidens and soft green helichrysums in this planter, which brightens the exterior of an old barn.

MATERIALS

76 cm (30 in) plastic window box
Compost
Slow-release plant food granules

PLANTS

3 scarlet pelargoniums
2 Bidens ferulifolia
2 red trailing verbenas
2 Helichrysum petiolare 'Aureum'

HELICHRYSUM

VERBENA

PELARGONIUM

BIDENS

GARDENER'S TIP

Regular dead-heading and an occasional foliar feed will keep the pelargoniums flowering prolifically all summer.

PLANT IN SPRING

1 The easiest way to open the drainage holes in a plastic planter is with an electric drill.

2 Fill the window box with compost, mixing in 2 teaspoons of slow-release plant food granules.

3 Plant the pelargoniums, evenly spaced, in the window box.

4 Plant the two bidens on either side of the central pelargonium to spill over the front of the planter.

5 Plant the two verbenas on either side of the central pelargonium towards the back of the planter.

6 Plant the helichrysums in the front corners. Water thoroughly and stand the box in a sunny position.

An Antique Wall Basket

This old wirework basket is an attractive container for a planting scheme which includes deep pink pansies, a variegated ivy-leaved pelargonium with soft pink flowers, a blue convolvulus and deep pink alyssum.

MATERIALS

30 cm (12 in) wall basket
Sphagnum moss
Compost
Slow-release plant food granules

PLANTS

5 rose-pink alyssum
Pelargonium 'L'Elégante'
3 deep pink pansies
Convolvulus sabatius

PELARGONIUM   ALYSSUM

CONVOLVULUS

PANSY

GARDENER'S TIP

Wall baskets look good among climbing plants, but you will need to trim the surrounding foliage if it gets too exuberant.

PLANT IN LATE SPRING OR
EARLY SUMMER

1 Line the back of the basket and the lower half of the front with moss. Plant the alyssum into the side by resting the rootballs on the moss, and guiding the foliage through the wires.

2 Line the remainder of the basket with moss and fill with compost, mixing a half-teaspoon of plant food granules into the top layer. Plant the pelargonium at the front of the basket.

3 Plant the pansies around the pelargonium. Plant the convolvulus at the back of the basket, trailing its foliage through the other plants. Water well and hang in partial sun.

A Cottage Terracotta Planter

Charming, cottage-garden plants tumble from this terracotta window box in a colourful display. The sunny flowers of the nemesias, marigolds and nasturtiums mingle with the cool, soft green helichrysums and blue-green nasturtium leaves.

MATERIALS

36 cm (14 in) terracotta window box
Crocks or other suitable drainage material
Compost
Slow-release plant food granules

PLANTS

3 pot marigolds (calendulas)
2 Helichrysum petiolare 'Aureum'
2 nasturtiums
2 Nemesia 'Orange Prince'

MARIGOLD

HELICHRYSUM

NASTURTIUM

NEMESIAS

1 Cover the base of the container with crocks and fill with compost, mixing in 2 teaspoons of plant food granules. Plant the marigolds along the back.

2 Plant the two helichrysums in the front corners of the window box.

3 Plant the nasturtiums between the marigolds at the back of the container.

4 Plant the nemesias between the helichrysums. Water well and stand in partial sun.

GARDENER'S TIP

The golden-leaved helichrysum retains a better colour if it is not in full sun all day. Too much sun makes it looks rather bleached.

PLANT IN SPRING

A Touch of Gold

Yellow lantana and the yellow-flowered variegated-leaf nasturtium provide colour from early summer onwards, and later in the season the black-eyed Susan will be covered in eye-catching flowers. Hang this exuberant basket high on a sunny wall so that the trailing plants can make as much growth as they like.

NASTURTIUM

BLACK-EYED
SUSAN

LANTANA

MATERIALS

30 cm (12 in) hanging basket
Sphagnum moss
Compost
Slow-release plant food granules

PLANTS

3 Alaska nasturtiums
Yellow lantana
3 black-eyed Susans (Thunbergia alata)

1 Line the lower half of the basket with moss.

2 Plant the nasturtiums into the side of the basket by resting the rootballs on the moss, and carefully guiding the leaves through the wires.

3 Line the rest of the basket with moss. Fill the basket with compost, mixing a teaspoon of slow-release plant food granules into the top layer.

4 Plant the lantana in the centre of the basket.

5 Plant the black-eyed Susans around the lantana. Water well and hang in a sunny position.

GARDENER'S TIP

Save some of the nasturtium seeds for next year's baskets and pots – they are among the easiest of plants to grow and some of the seeds are quite likely to find their own way into nearby cracks and crevices.

PLANT IN LATE SPRING OR EARLY SUMMER

A Wild One

Native plants are those that have grown
naturally in the countryside for thousands
of years. Some of the most colourful ones
are cornfield flowers, but many are quite
rare now. To enjoy them this summer, sow
a pot full of wild flowers to stand on
your doorstep.

FLOWER
POT

MATERIALS

Pebbles
Very large flower pot
Garden soil

WILD FLOWER
SEEDS

PLANTS

PEBBLES

Packet of wild flower seeds

GARDEN SOIL

GARDENER'S TIP

Remember to keep watering as the flowers grow!
Pots need much more watering than beds because the water drains away.

PLANT IN EARLY SPRING

1 Put a few pebbles in the base
of the pot for drainage.

2 Fill the pot with garden soil,
taking out any bits of roots or
large stones.

3 Make sure the surface is level,
then sprinkle a large pinch of
flower seeds evenly on top.

4 Cover the seeds lightly with
soil, just so you can't see them
any more, and water them in with
a gentle sprinkle.

A Pastel Composition

Pure white pelargonium blooms
emerge from a sea of blue
felicias, pinky-blue brachycome
daisies and
verbenas in
this romantic
basket.

PELARGONIUM

MATERIALS

36 cm (14 in) hanging basket
Sphagnum moss
Compost
Slow-release plant food granules

PLANTS

2 pink verbenas
2 Brachycome *'Pink Mist'*
Blue felicia
White pelargonium

VERBENA

BRACHYCOME

FELICIA

1 Line the basket with moss and
fill with compost, mixing a
teaspoon of slow-release plant
food granules into the top layer.

2 Plant the verbenas opposite
each other at the edge of the
basket, so that the foliage will
tumble over the sides.

3 Plant the brachycome daisies
around the edge of the basket.
Plant the felicia off-centre in the
middle of the basket.

4 Plant the pelargonium off-
centre in the remaining space
in the middle of the basket. Water
thoroughly and hang in a sunny
position.

GARDENER'S TIP

White pelargonium flowers
discolour as they age; be sure
to pick them off to keep
the basket looking at its best.

PLANT IN LATE SPRING OR
EARLY SUMMER

Daisy Chains

The soft yellow of the marguerites' flowers and foliage is emphasized by combining them with bright blue felicia in this summery basket.

MARGUERITE

HELICHRYSUM

FELICIA

MATERIALS

40 cm (16 in) hanging basket
Sphagnum moss
Compost
Slow-release plant food granules

PLANTS

3 variegated felicias
3 yellow marguerites
   (argyranthemums)
3 Helichrysum petiolare 'Aureum'

GARDENER'S TIP

Pinch out the growing tips
of the marguerites regularly to
encourage bushy plants.

PLANT IN LATE SPRING OR
EARLY SUMMER

1 Line the lower half of the basket with moss. Plant the felicias into the sides of the basket by resting the rootballs on the moss, and carefully guiding the foliage through the wires.

2 Line the rest of the basket with moss. Fill with compost, mixing a teaspoon of slow-release plant food granules into the top layer. Plant the marguerites in the top of the basket.

3 Plant the helichrysums between the marguerites, angling the plants to encourage them to grow over the edge of the basket. Water well and hang in full or partial sun.

Begonias and Fuchsias

Fuchsias are wonderful hanging basket plants as they flower prolifically late into the autumn. By the end of summer, when the other plants may start to look a bit straggly, the fuchsia will be at its best with a glorious display of colour.

MATERIALS

36 cm (14 in) hanging basket
Sphagnum moss
Compost
Slow-release plant
    food granules

PLANTS

2 Diascia 'Ruby Field'
3 Helichrysum microphyllum
Fuchsia 'Rose Winston' or
    similar soft pink
3 deep pink begonias

BEGONIA

DIASCIA

HELICHRYSUM

FUCHSIA

1 Line the lower half of the basket with moss and arrange the diascias and helichrysums in the basket to decide where to plant each one. Ensure they do not become tangled in the wires.

2 Plant the two diascias into the sides of the basket by resting the rootballs in the moss, and gently feeding the foliage through the wires.

GARDENER'S TIP

If some of the plants in the basket begin to look straggly in comparison with the fuchsia, cut them right back and give a liquid feed – they will grow with renewed vigour and provide a wonderful autumn show.

PLANT IN LATE SPRING OR
EARLY SUMMER

3 Line the rest of the basket with moss, partly fill with compost and plant the three helichrysums into the side of the basket near the rim.

4 Fill the basket with compost. Mix a teaspoon of slow-release plant food granules into the top layer of compost. Plant the fuchsia in the centre of the basket.

5 Finally, plant the three begonias around the fuchsia. Water well and hang the basket in full sun or partial shade.

Pot of Sunflowers

Sunflowers grow very well in pots provided you are not growing the giant varieties. Grow your own from seed; there are many kinds to choose from, including the one with double flowers used here.

MATERIALS

30 cm (12 in) glazed pot
Polystyrene or similar
  drainage material
Equal mix loam-based compost
  and container compost
Slow-release plant
  food granules

PLANTS

3 strong sunflower seedlings,
approximately 20 cm (8 in) tall

SUNFLOWER
SEEDLING

GARDENER'S TIP

Allow at least one of the sunflower heads to set seed. As the plant starts to die back, cut off the seedhead and hang it upside-down to ripen. Reserve some seeds for next year and then hang the seedhead outside for the birds.

PLANT SEEDS IN SPRING
AND SEEDLINGS IN SUMMER TO
FLOWER IN LATE SUMMER

1 Line the base of the pot with drainage material and fill with the compost mix. Scoop out evenly spaced holes for each seedling and plant, firming the compost around the plants.

2 Scatter 1 tablespoon of plant food granules on the surface of the compost. Place in a sunny position, out of the wind, and water regularly.

Alpine Sink

An old stone sink is a perfect container for a collection of alpine plants. The rock helps to create the effect of a miniature landscape and provides shelter for some of the plants. The sink is set up on the stand of an old sewing machine so that the plants can be admired easily.

MATERIALS

Stone sink or trough 76 x 50 cm (30 x 20 in)
Crocks or other suitable drainage material
Moss-covered rock
Loam-based compost with ⅓ added coarse grit
Washed gravel

PLANTS

Achillea tomentosa
Veronica peduncularis
Hebe
Ivy
Sedum ewersii
Aster natalensis
*Alpine willow (*Salix alpina*)*
Arabis ferdinandi-coburgi
  'Variegata'

1 Cover the drainage hole of the sink with crocks or other suitable drainage material. Position the rock. It is important to do this before adding the soil to create the effect of a natural rocky outcrop. Pour the compost into the sink.

2 Plan the position of your plants so that the end result will have a good balance of shape and colour. If the sink is very shallow you will need to scoop out the soil right to the base before planting but alpine plants are used to shallow soil. Make sure that the bottom leaves of low-growing plants are level with the soil. Too low and they will rot; too high and they will dry out.

3 When all the plants are in place, carefully pour washed gravel all around them to cover the whole soil area. Water and place in full or partial sun.

HEBE

SEDUM

ACHILLEA

VERONICA

IVY

Flowers for Late Summer

Although this window box is already looking good, towards the end of the summer it will really come into its own – by then the vibrant red and purple flowers of the pelargonium, salvias and lavenders will be at their most prolific.

MATERIALS

60 cm (24 in) wooden planter, stained black
Polystyrene or other suitable drainage material
Compost
Slow-release plant food granules

PLANTS

Pelargonium *'Tomcat'*
2 *Lavenders* (Lavandula pinnata)
2 Salvia *'Raspberry Royal'*
2 *blue brachycome daisies*
Convolvulus sabatius
6 *rose-pink alyssum*

ALYSSUM

CONVOLVULUS

BRACHYCOME

LAVENDER

SALVIA

PELARGONIUM

1 Line the base of the container with polystyrene or similar drainage material. Fill the window box with compost, mixing in 3 teaspoons of slow-release plant food granules. Plant the pelargonium at the back of the window box, in the centre.

2 Plant the two lavenders in the rear corners of the box.

3 Plant the salvias at the front on either side of the pelargonium.

4 Plant the brachycome daisies in the front corners of the window box.

5 Plant the convolvulus in the centre, in front of the pelargonium.

6 Fill the spaces with the alyssum. Water well and place in a sunny position.

GARDENER'S TIP

Both the lavenders and the salvias are highly aromatic, so if possible position this box near a door or a path, so that you can enjoy the fragrance as you brush against the plants.

PLANT IN EARLY SUMMER

Autumn Hanging Basket

Towards the end of the season the colours of summer hanging baskets do not always marry happily with the reds and golds of autumn. This is the time to plant a richly coloured hanging basket for winter.

MATERIALS

30 cm (12 in) hanging basket
Plastic pot
Sphagnum moss
Equal mix loam-based compost and container compost
Slow-release plant food granules

PLANTS

4 winter-flowering pansies
3 variegated ivies
Euonymus fortunei ('Emerald and Gold' was used here)
2 dahlias

DAHLIA

PANSY

IVY

EUONYMUS

GARDENER'S TIP

Although special composts with water-retaining gel are a boon for summer baskets, they can get waterlogged in the cooler months. Mix equal parts of loam-based and container composts for autumn and winter planting.

PLANT IN SPRING OR SUMMER TO FLOWER IN AUTUMN

1 Support the hanging basket on a pot. Unhook the chain from one fixing point so that it hangs down one side of the basket. Line the base and bottom half of the basket with a generous layer of sphagnum moss.

2 Pour in compost until it is level with the top of the moss. Plant your first layer of three pansies and three ivies, passing the foliage through the wire of the basket, so that the rootballs of the plants are resting on the compost.

3 Line the rest of the basket with moss and top up with compost, firming it around the roots of the ivies and pansies. Then plant the remaining plants in the top of the basket, with the euonymus in the centre and the remaining pansy and dahlias surrounding it. Scatter a tablespoon of slow-release plant food granules on to the compost and water the hanging basket well. Re-attach the chain and hang the basket in full or partial sun.

Heather Window Box

This is a perfect project for an absolute beginner as it is extremely simple to achieve. The bark window box is a sympathetic container for the heathers, which look quite at home in their bed of moss.

MATERIALS

30 cm (12 in) bark window box
Crocks or other suitable drainage material
Ericaceous compost
Bun moss

PLANTS

Heathers

HEATHERS

1 Put a layer of crocks or other suitable drainage material in the bottom of the box.

2 Remove the heathers from their pots and position them in the window box.

3 Fill the gaps between the plants with the compost, pressing it around the plants. Water in well.

4 Tuck the bun moss snugly around the plants so that no soil is visible. Place in full or partial sun.

GARDENER'S TIP

Do not be tempted to use ordinary compost as it contains lime which, with a very few exceptions, is not suitable for the majority of heathers.

PLANT IN AUTUMN

Evergreens with Extra Colour

They may be easy to look after but all-year-round window boxes can start to look a bit lifeless after a couple of seasons. It does not take much trouble to add a few seasonal flowers and it makes all the difference to a display.

MATERIALS

76 cm (30 in) plastic window
  box
Compost
Slow-release plant food granules

PLANTS

Hebe *'Baby Marie'*
Convolvulus cneorum
Potentilla *'Nunk'*
Variegated ivies
2 Diascia *'Ruby Field'*
Pink marguerite (Argyranthemum
  'Flamingo')

IVY

CONVOLVULUS

POTENTILLA

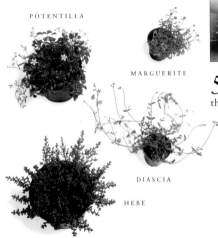

MARGUERITE

DIASCIA

HEBE

1 Check the drainage holes are open in the base and, if not, drill or punch them open. Fill the window box with compost, mixing in 3 teaspoons of slow-release plant food granules. Plant the hebe in the centre.

2 Plant the convolvulus near one end of the window box.

3 Plant the potentilla near the other end of the window box.

4 Plant the two ivies at the front corners of the window box.

5 Plant the diascias on either side of the hebe at the front of the window box.

6 Plant the marguerite between the hebe and the convolvulus at the back. Water well and stand in full or partial sun.

GARDENER'S TIP

At the end of the summer, remove the diascias and marguerite, feed the remaining plants with more granules, and fill the spaces with winter-flowering plants such as pansies or heathers.

PLANT IN SPRING

Classic Topiary

MATERIALS

4 large terracotta pots
Bark chippings
Crocks or other suitable drainage
  material
Equal mix loam-based compost
  and container compost
Slow-release plant food granules

PLANTS

4 box trees (Buxus sempervirens)
in different topiary shapes

BOX TREES (*BUXUS SEMPERVIRENS*)

The clean lines of the topiary are matched by the simplicity of the terracotta pots. Since the eye is drawn to the outlines of the box plants, decorated pots would be a distraction.

1 If the plant has been well looked after in the nursery it may not need potting on yet. In this case simply slip the plant in its pot into the terracotta container.

2 To conserve moisture and conceal the plastic pot, cover with a generous layer of bark chippings.

3 To repot a box tree, first place a good layer of crocks or other drainage material in the bottom of the pot. Remove the tree from its plastic pot and place it in the terracotta container. Surround the rootball with compost, pushing it well down the sides.

4 Scatter a tablespoon of plant food granules on the surface of the compost and top with a layer of bark chippings. Water well and position in sun or partial shade.

GARDENER'S TIP

Don't get carried away when you trim topiary. Little and often, with an ordinary pair of scissors, is better than occasional dramatic gestures with a pair of shears.

PLANT AT ANY
TIME OF THE YEAR

Trug of Winter Pansies

Winter pansies are wonderfully resilient and will bloom bravely throughout the winter as long as they are regularly dead-headed. This trug may be moved around to provide colour wherever it is needed, and acts as a perfect antidote to mid-winter gloom.

MATERIALS

Old wooden trug
Sphagnum moss
Compost
Slow-release plant food granules

PLANTS

15 winter-flowering pansies (violas)

PANSIES

1 Line the trug with a generous layer of sphagnum moss. Fill the moss lining with compost.

2 Plant the pansies by starting at one end and filling the spaces between the plants with compost as you go. Gently firm each plant into position and add a final layer of compost mixed with a tablespoon of plant food granules around the pansies. Water and place in a fairly sunny position.

GARDENER'S TIP

Not everyone has an old trug available, but an old basket, colander, or an enamel bread bin could be used instead. Junk shops and flea markets are a great source of containers that are too battered for their original use, but fine for planting.

PLANT IN AUTUMN TO FLOWER IN WINTER

Evergreen Garden

Evergreen plants come in many shapes, sizes and shades. Grouped in containers they will provide you with year-round interest and colour.

MATERIALS

Terracotta pots of various sizes
Crocks or similar drainage
  material
Equal mix loam-based compost
  and container compost
Plant saucers
Gravel
Slow-release plant food granules

PLANTS

False cypress (Chamaecyparis
  lawsoniana *'Columnaris'*; C.
  pisifera *'Filifera Aurea'*)
Berberis darwinii
Berberis thunbergii *'Atropurpurea*
  Nana'
Pachysandra terminalis
Bergenia

FALSE CYPRESS

BERGENIA

PACHYSANDRA

BERBERIS

GARDENER'S TIP

Include some golden or variegated foliage amongst your evergreens and choose contrasting leaf forms to make a striking group.

PLANT AT ANY
TIME OF THE YEAR

1 Large shrubs, such as this conifer, should be potted into a proportionally large container. Place plenty of crocks or similar drainage material at the base of the pot. If the plant is at all potbound, tease the roots loose before planting in its new pot. Fill around the rootball with compost, pressing it down firmly around the edges of the pot.

2 Smaller plants, like bergenia, should be planted in a pot slightly larger than the existing one. Place crocks in the base of the pot, position the plant and then fill around the edges with compost. Repeat with the remaining plants.

3 Plants will stay moist longer if they are stood in saucers of wet gravel. This group of plants will do well positioned in partial shade. Water regularly and feed with slow-release plant food granules in the spring and autumn.

Year-round Window Box

In the same way that a garden has certain plants that provide structure throughout the year, this window box has been planted so that there is always plenty of foliage. Extra colour may be introduced each season by including small flowering plants, such as heathers.

MATERIALS

90 cm (3 ft) wooden window box, preferably self-watering
Equal mix loam-based compost and container compost
Slow-release plant food granules
Bark chippings

PLANTS

Skimmia reevesiana 'Rubella'
2 Arundinaria pygmaea
2 Cotoneaster conspicuus
2 periwinkles (Vinca minor 'Variegata')
6 heathers

PERIWINKLE

COTONEASTER   SKIMMIA

ARUNDINARIA

HEATHER

1 If you are using a self-watering container, feed the wicks through the base of the plastic liner. Slip the liner into the wooden window box.

2 Before you start planting, plan the position of the plants so that the colours and shapes look well balanced. Remove the plants from their pots, tease loose their roots if they look at all potbound and position in the window box. Top up with compost.

3 Once the structure plants are in place you can add the colour; in this case, the heathers. Scoop out a hole for each heather and then plant, pressing firmly around each one. Scatter two tablespoons of plant food granules over the surface.

4 Top-dress the window box with a layer of bark chippings; this will help to conserve moisture. Water thoroughly.

GARDENER'S TIP

Plants do not need watering in winter, unless they are sheltered from the rain. Even then they should be watered sparingly and not in frosty weather. Self-watering containers should be drained before winter to prevent frost damage.

PLANT AT ANY
TIME OF THE YEAR

Winter Cheer

Many window boxes are left unplanted through the winter, but you can soon brighten the house or garden during this season with an easy arrangement of pot-grown plants plunged in bark.

MATERIALS

40 cm (16 in) glazed window box
Bark chippings

PLANTS

2 miniature conifers
2 variegated ivies
2 red polyanthus

POLYANTHUS   CONIFER

IVY

1 Water all the plants. Place the conifers, still in their pots, at each end of the window box.

2 Half-fill the window box with bark chippings.

3 Place the pots of polyanthus on the bark chippings between the two conifers.

4 Place the pots of ivy in the front corners of the window box. Add further bark chippings to the container until all the pots are concealed. Water only when plants show signs of dryness. Stand in any position.

GARDENER'S TIP

When it is time to replant the window box, plunge the conifers, still in their pots, in a shady position in the garden. Water well through the spring and summer and they may be used again next year.

PLANT IN EARLY WINTER

Classic Winter Colours

Convolvulus cneorum is an attractive small shrub with eye-catching silver-grey leaves, which last through winter, and white flowers in spring and summer. Planted with ice-blue pansies, it makes a softly subtle display from autumn to spring.

MATERIALS

30 cm (12 in) hanging basket
Sphagnum moss
Compost

PLANTS

8 silver/blue pansies (Viola
'Silver Wings', or similar)
Convolvulus cneorum

CONVOLVULUS

PANSIES

1 Half-line the basket with moss and fill with compost to the top of the moss. Plant four of the pansies into the side of the basket by placing their rootballs on the compost, and gently guiding the leaves through the side of the basket.

2 Line the rest of the basket with moss and top up with compost. Plant the convolvulus in the centre of the basket.

GARDENER'S TIP

At the end of the winter cut back any dead wood or straggly branches on the *Convolvulus cneorum*, and give a liquid feed to encourage new growth. Small shrubs such as this may be used in hanging baskets for one season, but will then need planting into a larger container or the border.

PLANT IN AUTUMN

3 Plant the remaining four pansies around the convolvulus. Water well and hang in sun or partial shade.

Gothic Ivy

Twisted willow branches set into a chimney pot offer an attractive support for ivy, and will provide welcome interest in the winter.

MATERIALS

Chimney pot
Compost
90 cm (3 ft) wire netting

PLANTS

4–5 branches of twisted willow
Large ivy (Hedera helix var. hibernica was used here)

IVY

1 Place the chimney pot in its final position (in shade or half-shade) and half-fill with compost. Fold or crumple the wire netting and push down into the chimney pot so that it rests on the compost.

2 Arrange the willow branches in the chimney pot, pushing the stems through the wire netting.

3 Rest the ivy, in its pot, on the wire netting amongst the willow branches. Fill the chimney pot with compost to within 10 cm (4 in) of the rim. Cut loose any ties and remove the cane.

4 Arrange the stems of ivy over the willow branches and water. To start with it may look rather contrived, but as the ivy settles into its new surroundings it will attach itself to the willow.

GARDENER'S TIP

You may find that some of your twisted willow branches take root in the compost. Plant a rooted branch in the garden where it will grow into a tree. It will eventually be quite large so do not plant it near the house.

PLANT AT ANY
TIME OF THE YEAR

Golden Christmas Holly

Evergreen standard holly trees are splendid container plants. This golden holly in a gilded pot has been dressed up for Christmas with bows and baubles.

HOLLY

MATERIALS

40 cm (16 in) terracotta pot
Gold spray-paint
Crocks or similar drainage material
Composted manure
Loam-based compost
Pine cones
90 cm (3 ft) wired ribbon
Tin Christmas decorations

PLANTS

Golden holly

1 Spray the pot with gold paint and leave to dry. Place a good layer of crocks or similar drainage material in the base. Cover with a 7.5 cm (3 in) layer of composted manure and a thin layer of loam-based potting compost. Remove the holly from its existing container and place in the gilded pot.

2 Surround the rootball with compost, pressing down firmly to ensure that the tree is firmly planted, and cover the surface with pine cones.

3 Tie the ribbon into a bow around the trunk of the tree. Spray the decorations gold and hang in the branches. Water the tree to settle it in, but do not do this on a frosty day.

GARDENER'S TIP

In the autumn, plant some corms of *Iris reticulata* or similar small bulbs in the compost surrounding the tree for a delightful spring display.

PLANT IN AUTUMN, WINTER OR SPRING

An Evergreen Wall Basket

Pansies will flower throughout
the winter. Even if they are
flattened by rain, frost or
snow, at the first sign of
improvement in the weather
their heads will pop up again
to bring brightness to the
dullest day. They have been
planted with ivies to provide
colour from early autumn
through to late spring.

MATERIALS

30 cm (12 in) wall basket
Sphagnum moss
Compost

PLANTS

2 golden variegated ivies
2 copper pansies (viola)
Yellow pansy (viola)

PANSIES

IVY

GARDENER'S TIP

Winter baskets do not need regular
feeding and should only be
watered in very dry conditions.
To prolong the flowering life of the
pansies, dead-head regularly and
pinch out any straggly stems to
encourage new shoots from the base.

PLANT IN AUTUMN

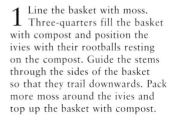

1 Line the basket with moss.
Three-quarters fill the basket
with compost and position the
ivies with their rootballs resting
on the compost. Guide the stems
through the sides of the basket
so that they trail downwards. Pack
more moss around the ivies and
top up the basket with compost.

2 Plant the two copper pansies
at either end of the basket.

3 Plant the yellow pansy in the
centre. Water well and hang in
shade or semi-shade.

Edible Collections

*What could be nicer than reaching out of the kitchen window to gather fresh herbs
from the window-sill, or eating succulent tomatoes or strawberries grown on
the balcony? If you don't have room for a vegetable patch, even if you don't have
a garden at all, you can still enjoy home-grown produce if you plant it in containers.
Go for compact varieties of beans and tomatoes, and choose lettuces such as
'Salad Bowl' so that you can pick just what you need and leave the plants to go on
growing. You will be able to grow a wide range: you could even try a few early
potatoes in a pot, for the first and most delicious crop of the year.*

*Kitchen-garden containers can be beautiful, too. Alpine strawberries are both
decorative and delicious tumbling out of a hanging basket, and you can grow
herbs for their looks as well as their flavour, choosing variegated mints, red-leaved
basil or purple sage to contribute to the visual feast.*

ABOVE: *Herbs thrive on a sunny windowsill.*

Herbs in the Shade

Although the Mediterranean herbs need lots of sunshine, there are many others which prefer a cooler situation to look and taste their best. This window box, ideal for just outside the kitchen door or window, has an interesting variety of mints, sorrel, chives, lemon balm and parsley.

MATERIALS

50 cm (20 in) terracotta window box
Polystyrene or other suitable drainage material
Compost
Slow-release plant food granules, pelleted chicken manure, or similar organic plant food

PLANTS

Lemon balm
3 mints (black peppermint, silver mint and curly spearmint were used here)
Sorrel
Chives
Parsley

LEMON BALM

MINTS

CHIVE

SORREL

PARSLEY   MINT

1 Line the base of the container with polystyrene or similar drainage material. Top up with compost, mixing in 3 teaspoons of slow-release plant food granules or organic alternative.

2 Plant the lemon balm and two of the mints along the back of the window box.

3 Plant the third mint, the sorrel and the chives along the front. Finally, plant the parsley in the centre. Position the box in light shade and water thoroughly.

GARDENER'S TIP

Use the freshly picked mint to make refreshing teas. Pour hot boiled water over a few washed leaves and infuse for five minutes.

PLANT IN EARLY SPRING

Vital Ingredients

A lovely present for an enthusiastic cook, this window box contains chervil, coriander, fennel, garlic, purple sage, French tarragon, savory, origanum and basil.

MATERIALS

45 cm (18 in) wooden window
  box
Crocks or other suitable drainage
  material
Compost
Slow-release plant food granules,
  pelleted chicken manure, or
  similar organic plant food

PLANTS

French tarragon
Chervil
Garlic
Coriander
Purple sage
Basil
Fennel
Savory
Origanum

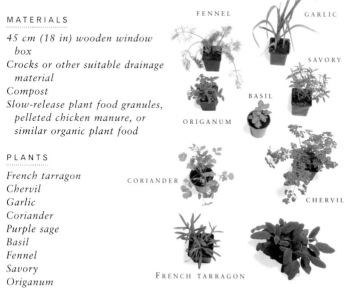

FENNEL   GARLIC

SAVORY

BASIL

ORIGANUM

CORIANDER

CHERVIL

FRENCH TARRAGON

PURPLE SAGE

GARDENER'S TIP

There are now various kinds of basil seed available (some specialists sell at least 12), with varieties ranging from Greek to Indonesian. The key point when growing them is to remove the flower buds the moment they appear as the leaves will quickly lose their flavour once the flowers open.

PLANT IN SPRING

1 Line the base of the container with crocks or other suitable drainage material. Fill the window box with compost, mixing in a teaspoon of slow-release plant food granules or an organic alternative.

2 Before planting the herbs, arrange them in the window box in their pots.

3 Plant the back row of herbs in the window box first.

4 Plant more herbs at the front of the window box. Water well and stand in a sunny position.

Wine Case Herb Garden

Add a coat of varnish to an old wine case to make an attractive and durable container for a miniature herb garden. The container can be placed near the kitchen door or on a balcony.

MATERIALS

Wooden wine case
Pliers
Sandpaper
Paintbrush
Light oak semi-matt varnish
Crocks or similar drainage
   material
Compost with 1/3 added coarse
   grit
Slow-release plant food granules
   or pelleted chicken manure
Bark chippings

PLANTS

Selection of 7 herbs, such as sage, chives, parsley, mint, tarragon, lemon thyme and creeping thyme

SAGE

PARSLEY

CHIVES

GARDENER'S TIP

Some herbs like cool, partial shade while others like hot, dry, free-draining soil. A mixed herb garden will thrive for only one growing season.

PLANT IN SPRING

1 Remove any wire staples from around the edges of the box and sand down the rough edges. Apply two coats of varnish on the inside and outside of the box, allowing the varnish to dry thoroughly between coats. When dry, cover the base of the box with a layer of crocks or similar drainage material.

2 Before planting, decide how you are going to arrange the plants in the container to achieve a pleasing balance of colour, height and shape.

3 Fill the box with gritty compost and plant from one end of the box to the other. Loosen the rootballs, as this will help the plants to root into the surrounding compost.

4 When the planting is complete, scatter 2 tablespoons of plant food granules or pelleted chicken manure on the surface of the compost. Firm in the plants and mulch with bark chippings to retain moisture. Water well.

The Good Life

This window box will not exactly make you self-sufficient, but it is surprising how many different vegetables can be grown in a small space. It is perfect for anyone who likes the taste of home-grown vegetables but does not have a garden to grow them in.

MATERIALS

76 cm (30 in) plastic window box
Compost
Slow-release plant food granules, pelleted chicken manure or similar organic plant food

PLANTS

Garlic
3 Chinese leaves
4 plugs of beetroot (see Gardener's Tip)
Pepper plant
3 dwarf French beans
3 plugs of shallots

BEETROOT

CHINESE LEAVES

GARLIC

FRENCH BEAN

PEPPER

SHALLOTS

1 Check the drainage holes are open in the container's base. Fill the window box with compost, mixing in 2 teaspoons of slow-release plant food granules or an organic alternative. Start planting from one end.

2 Starting at the right-hand end of the window box, first plant the garlic. Next plant the Chinese leaves.

3 Follow these with the plugs of beetroot.

4 Plant the pepper plant next, just to the left of the centre.

5 Now plant the three dwarf French bean plants.

6 Finally, plant the shallot plugs in the left-hand corner. Water well and stand in full or partial sun.

GARDENER'S TIP

It is now possible to buy plugs of small vegetable plants at garden centres. There is no need to separate the plants provided there is sufficient room between the clumps.

PLANT IN SPRING

A Taste for Flowers

It is often said that something "looks good enough to eat", and in this instance it is true. All the flowers in this window box may be used for flavour and garnishes.

MATERIALS

36 cm (14 in) terracotta window box
Crocks or other suitable drainage material
Compost
Slow-release plant food granules, pelleted chicken manure or similar organic plant food

PLANTS

Chives
2 nasturtiums
2 pansies (viola) with well-marked "faces"
2 pot marigolds (calendula)

CHIVE

NASTURTIUM

PANSY

MARIGOLDS

GARDENER'S TIP

To keep all the plants producing flowers, dead-head regularly. Once a plant has set seed it considers its work done and will produce fewer and fewer flowers.

PLANT IN EARLY SPRING

1 Cover the base of the window box with a layer of crocks or similar drainage material. Fill with compost, mixing in 2 teaspoons of slow-release plant food granules or an organic alternative. Plant the chives in the right-hand corner.

2 Plant one of the nasturtiums in the left-hand corner and the other centre-front.

3 Plant one pansy at the back next to the chives, and the other at the front to the left of the central nasturtium.

4 Plant one of the marigolds at the back between the pansy and nasturtium, and the other one just behind the central nasturtium.

A Hanging Garden of Herbs

A basket of herbs is both decorative and useful, especially when hung near the kitchen door or window. Herbs benefit from regular picking to encourage the plants to produce lots of tender new shoots throughout the summer. Some herbs can be very vigorous so be sure to choose compact varieties for your hanging basket.

MATERIALS

30 cm (12 in) hanging basket
Sphagnum moss
Compost
Slow-release plant food granules

PLANTS

5 parsley
French tarragon
Sage
Rosemary (prostrate form)
2 basil

PARSLEY

FRENCH TARRAGON

BASIL

ROSEMARY

SAGE

GARDENER'S TIP

Fortunately, the strongly aromatic nature of most herbs does dissuade pests, but if you should have any problems be sure to use a safe organic pesticide. Soapy washing-up water can be used against greenfly.

PLANT IN SPRING

1 Line the lower half of the basket with moss. Plant the parsley, resting the rootballs on the moss and feeding the leaves through the sides of the basket.

2 Line the rest of the basket with moss and fill with compost. Mix a teaspoon of slow-release plant food granules into the top. Plant the tarragon.

3 Plant the sage. Plant the prostrate rosemary, angling it slightly to encourage it to grow over the side of the basket.

4 Finally, plant the two basil plants and water well before hanging in partial sun. A regular liquid feed is recommended.

Butler's Tray Kitchen Garden

Not many of us have the space or time to maintain a kitchen garden, but this table-top selection of plants will give you a taste of the delights to be had, and might even inspire you to try the real thing.

MATERIALS

Terracotta pots of various sizes
Crocks or other suitable drainage
* material*
Compost
Butler's tray
Thick plastic sheet
Clay granules

PLANTS

Selection of kitchen garden plants, such as pot marigolds (calendula), basil, nasturtium, miniature tomato, strawberry and French tarragon

STRAWBERRY

TARRAGON

TOMATO

NASTURTIUM

BASIL   MARIGOLD

1 If the plants have well-developed root systems, like this marigold, they will benefit from being planted in a larger pot. Place crocks in the bottom of the pots for drainage. Gently tease loose some of the roots before you repot the plant.

2 You may be able to divide a single basil plant when repotting, enabling you to fill two pots. The miniature tomato and the strawberry should be planted in larger pots to allow plenty of room for root development.

3 Nasturtiums flower better in poor soil. Once you have planted them, leave them to their own devices. Give them a little water but no plant food or you will get lots of leaves and very few flowers.

4 Line your tray with a thick plastic sheet and cover it with clay granules. These retain moisture and create a damp micro-climate for the plants. Arrange your plants on the tray, place in a sunny position and water and feed (except the nasturtiums) regularly.

GARDENER'S TIP

The marigolds and nasturtiums are not purely decorative, the flowers and leaves of both are edible and can be used in salads.

PLANT IN LATE SPRING OR EARLY SUMMER

Beans and Parsley in a Basket

A hanging basket planted with dwarf beans and parsley can be surprisingly productive and will outwit all but the most acrobatic of snails.

MATERIALS

36 cm (14 in) hanging basket
Sphagnum moss
Compost
Slow-release plant food granules

PLANTS

7 parsley plants
3 dwarf bean plants

PARSLEY

DWARF BEAN

1 Line the lower half of the basket with moss and half-fill with compost.

2 Plant the parsley into the sides of the basket, resting the root-balls on the compost and feeding the leaves through the wires.

3 Gently separate the bean plants from one another.

4 Line the upper half of the basket with moss and add more compost. Mix a teaspoon of slow-release plant food granules into the top layer. Plant the beans in the compost. Water the basket thoroughly and hang in partial sun.

GARDENER'S TIP

Fruit and vegetable hanging baskets need quite a lot of attention to crop well. They should be kept moist at all times and need a liquid feed once a week. If you are going to be away, move the basket into the shade, where it will not dry out so quickly.

PLANT IN SPRING

Wild Strawberry Basket

Wild strawberries can be grown in a basket and enjoyed anywhere, whether in the countryside or a small city garden.

MATERIALS

30 cm (12 in) square wire basket
Sphagnum moss
*Equal mix loam-based compost
  and container compost*
*Slow-release plant food granules
  or organic plant food*

PLANTS

*4 alpine
strawberry plants*

ALPINE
STRAWBERRY

1 Line the base and sides of the basket with a generous layer of sphagnum moss.

2 Fill the lined area with compost. Scoop out a hollow for each strawberry plant, and press the compost firmly around the rootball as you plant.

3 Scatter a tablespoon of plant food granules on the surface of the compost.

4 Tuck more moss around the edges and under the leaves to conserve moisture and stop the fruit touching the soil. Water and place in full or partial sun.

GARDENER'S TIP

Propagate strawberry runners by pinning the plantlets into small pots of compost. A loop of wire or a hairpin placed on either side of the plantlet will hold it firmly in place until it has rooted. Then simply cut the runner and you have a new strawberry plant.

PLANT IN SPRING TO FRUIT
IN SUMMER

Good Enough to Eat

All the plants in this basket bear an edible crop: the tomato fruit, nasturtium flowers and parsley leaves. You could even impress your family or guests with a "hanging basket salad", using all three together.

MATERIALS

36 cm (14 in) hanging basket
Sphagnum moss
Compost
Slow-release plant food granules

PLANTS

6 parsley plants
3 trailing nasturtiums
3 'Tumbler' tomatoes, or similar

PARSLEY

TRAILING
NASTURTIUM

TOMATO

GARDENER'S TIP

If you would prefer to grow your plants organically, plant this basket using an organic compost and use natural plant foods such as pelleted chicken manure or a liquid seaweed feed.

PLANT IN LATE SPRING OR
EARLY SUMMER

1 Line the lower half of the basket with moss.

2 Plant three parsley plants into the side of the basket by resting the rootballs on the moss, and feeding the leaves through the side of the basket.

3 Line the basket to just below the rim and fill with compost. Mix a teaspoon of slow-release plant food granules into the top of the compost. Plant three nasturtium plants into the side of the basket, just below the rim.

4 Finish lining the basket with moss, being careful to tuck plenty of moss around the nasturtiums.

5 Plant the tomato plants in the top of the basket.

6 Plant the remaining three parsley plants amongst the tomatoes in the top of the basket. Water well and hang in a sunny position. Liquid feed regularly.

Summer Fruits

The red of ripening strawberries is matched by vibrant red pelargonium flowers in this unusual arrangement. Alpine strawberry plants make a good contrast, with their delicate fruit and tendrils.

ALPINE
STRAWBERRY

STRAWBERRY

PELARGONIUM

MATERIALS

36 cm (14 in) hanging basket
Sphagnum moss
Compost
Slow-release plant food granules
  or organic plant food

PLANTS

3 'Maxim' strawberry plants, or
  similar
Pelargonium 'Miss Flora', or
  similar
3 alpine strawberry plants

1 Line the basket with moss.

2 Fill the basket with compost. Mix a teaspoon of slow-release plant food granules into the top layer of compost. Plant the strawberry plants around the side of the basket.

3 Plant the pelargonium in the centre of the basket.

4 Plant the alpine strawberries in between the larger strawberry plants. Water well, and hang in partial or full sun.

GARDENER'S TIP

After the large strawberries have fruited, cut back all their foliage to encourage the formation of next year's flowers. The pelargonium and alpine strawberries will stop the basket looking too bare while the new foliage is growing.

PLANT IN SPRING

Home-grown Salads

These compact but heavy-fruiting tomato plants have been specially bred to be grown in containers. Teamed with lettuce, radishes, chives and parsley, they provide all the ingredients for a fresh garden salad.

GARDENER'S TIP

Keep the tomato plants watered at all times, and liquid feed with a proprietary tomato food or liquid seaweed fertilizer.

PLANT IN SPRING

MATERIALS

76 cm (30 in) plastic window box
Compost
Slow-release plant food granules, pelleted chicken manure or similar organic plant food

PLANTS

3 'Tumbler' tomatoes
Chives
4 lettuces, 'Little Gem' or 'Corsair'
2 'Salad Bowl' lettuces
4 parsley plants
Radish seed

TOMATO

LETTUCE

CHIVES

LETTUCE

PARSLEY

1 Check the drainage holes are open in the base of the window box and, if not, drill or punch them open. Fill with compost, mixing in 2 teaspoons of slow-release plant food granules or organic alternative. Plant the tomatoes, evenly spaced, along the centre.

2 Plant the chives in front of the middle tomato plant. Plant the 'Little Gem' or 'Corsair' lettuces diagonally to one another between the tomato plants.

3 Plant the 'Salad Bowl' lettuces in the front corners. Plant the parsley plants diagonally opposite one another alongside the 'Little Gem' or 'Corsair' lettuces.

4 Scatter radish seed between the plants and gently rake into the soil. Water thoroughly and stand in a sunny position.

Scented
Collections

Scent gives a lovely extra dimension to container planting schemes, especially for planters that are sited at "nose" level, such as window boxes. On warm days the aromas will drift in through open windows. Use plants with scented leaves for a really lasting effect: herbs such as lavender and mint are invaluable foils for larger-flowered plants and will fill the air with fragrance. The scented-leaf pelargoniums are perfect container plants and you can choose from a wide variety of lovely variegations and leaf shapes as well as perfumes that range from lemon and mint to rose. Their charming pink flowers are an added bonus. Put scented plants in containers near paths and doorways, where their rich fragrances will be released each time you brush past them. A fragrant plant in a pot by the front door makes a special welcome for visitors.

ABOVE: *Lavender is always a favourite for its delightful scent. Here it is combined with scaevolas and trailing convolvulus.*

Scented Window Box

The soft silvers and blues of the flowers and foliage beautifully complement this verdigris window box. The scent of the lavender and petunias will drift magically through open windows.

MATERIALS

60 cm (24 in) window box
Gravel or similar drainage material
Equal mix loam-based compost and container compost
Slow-release plant food granules

PLANTS

2 lavenders
2 pale blue petunias
4 deep blue petunias
4 Chaenorhinum glareosum (or lilac lobelia)
6 Helichrysum petiolare

PETUNIA

CHAENORHINUM

HELICHRYSUM

LAVENDER

GARDENER'S TIP

To keep a densely planted container like this looking its best it is necessary to feed regularly with a liquid feed, or more simply to mix slow-release plant food granules into the surface of the compost to last the whole summer. Cut back the lavender heads after flowering to ensure bushy flowering plants again next year.

PLANT IN LATE SPRING OR EARLY SUMMER

1 Fill the bottom 5 cm (2 in) of the window box with drainage material and half-fill with compost. Position the lavender plants, loosening the soil around the roots before planting, as they will establish better this way.

2 Now arrange the flowering plants around the lavender, leaving spaces for the helichrysums between them.

3 Finally, add the helichrysums and fill between the plants with compost, pressing firmly so that no air gaps are left around the roots. Place in a sunny position and water regularly.

A Nose-twitcher Window Box

One of the French country names for the nasturtium means 'nose-twitcher' and refers to the peppery smell of the plant. It has been planted here with the equally aromatic and colourful ginger mint and pot marigold.

MATERIALS

25 cm (10 in) terracotta window box
Crocks or other suitable drainage material
Compost
Slow-release plant food granules

PLANTS

Variegated ginger mint
Nasturtium, Tropaeolum 'Empress of India',
  or similar
Pot marigold (Calendula 'Gitana', or similar)

MARIGOLD

NASTURTIUM

GINGER MINT

GARDENER'S TIP
A small window box like this one can double as a table-centre for an outdoor meal.

PLANT IN SPRING

1 Cover the base of the window box with a layer of crocks or similar drainage material. Fill the container with compost, mixing in a half-teaspoon of slow-release plant food granules.

2 Plant the ginger mint on the right of the container.

3 Plant the nasturtium in the centre.

4 Plant the marigold on the left of the container. Water well and stand in full or partial sun.

Sweet-smelling Summer Flowers

Scented pelargonium and verbena are combined with heliotrope and petunias to make a window box that is fragrant as well as a visual pleasure.

MATERIALS

40cm (16 in) terracotta window box
Crocks or other suitable drainage material
Compost
Slow-release plant food granules

PLANTS

Scented-leaf Pelargonium *'Lady Plymouth'*
3 soft pink petunias
Heliotrope
2 Verbena *'Pink Parfait'*

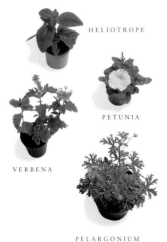

HELIOTROPE

PETUNIA

VERBENA

PELARGONIUM

GARDENER'S TIP

At the end of the summer the pelargonium can be potted up and kept through the winter as a houseplant. Reduce the height of the plant by at least a half and it will soon send out new shoots.

PLANT IN LATE SPRING OR EARLY SUMMER

1 Cover the base of the window box with a layer of crocks. Fill with compost, mixing in 2 teaspoons of slow-release plant food granules. Plant the pelargonium to the right of centre, towards the back of the window box.

2 Plant a petunia in each corner and one in the centre at the front of the window box.

3 Plant the heliotrope to the left of the pelargonium.

4 Plant one verbena behind the heliotrope and the other in front of the pelargonium. Water well and place in a sunny position.

Sweet-scented Lavender

In this large basket an unusual lavender is planted amongst *Convolvulus sabatius* and the fan-shaped flowers of scaevola in cool, toning shades of blue. Underplanting with trailing plants ensures that the flowers cascade down the sides of the basket.

MATERIALS

40 cm (16 in) hanging basket
Sphagnum moss
Compost
Slow-release plant food granules

PLANTS

3 Convolvulus sabatius
2 *scaevolas*
2 *lavenders* (Lavandula
    dentata *var.* candicans)

LAVENDER

CONVOLVULUS

SCAEVOLA

1 Line the lower half of the basket with moss.

2 Plant two of the convolvulus into the side of the basket by resting the rootballs on the moss, and carefully guiding the foliage between the wires.

3 Plant one of the scaevolas into the side of the basket in the same way.

4 Line the rest of the basket with moss, taking care to tuck it around the underplanting.

5 Fill the basket with compost, mixing a teaspoon of slow-release plant food granules into the top layer. Plant the lavenders opposite one another in the top.

6 Plant the remaining convolvulus and scaevola plants in the spaces between the lavenders. Water thoroughly and hang in a sunny position.

GARDENER'S TIP

If you are unable to obtain *Lavandula dentata*, the varieties called 'Hidcote' or 'Munstead' are readily available and make suitable substitutes.

PLANT IN SPRING

Scented Pelargoniums

There is a wonderful variation in leaf size, shape and colouring, as well as an incredible diversity of scents, amongst the *Pelargonium* family. Choose the fragrances you like best and put the plants where you will brush against them to release their fragrance.

MATERIALS

40 cm (16 in) terracotta window box
Crocks or other suitable drainage material
Compost
Slow-release plant food granules

PLANTS

4 scented-leaf pelargoniums

PELARGONIUMS

GARDENER'S TIP

During the summer, pick and dry the leaves of these pelargoniums for use in pot-pourri or in muslin bags to scent linen. If you have a greenhouse or conservatory, move the window box inside for the winter and water sparingly until spring.

PLANT IN SPRING

1 Cover the base of the window box with a layer of crocks or other suitable drainage material. Fill with compost, mixing in 2 teaspoons of slow-release plant food granules. Plant the first pelargonium at the right-hand end of the container.

2 Choose a plant with contrasting leaf colour and shape, and place this next to the first pelargonium towards the front edge of the window box.

3 Plant the third pelargonium behind the second.

4 Finally, plant the fourth pelargonium at the left-hand end of the container. Water well and position in full or partial sun.

A Butterfly Garden

We should all do our bit to encourage butterflies into our gardens and this window box filled with sedum, marjoram, thyme and origanum should prove irresistible. All these plants are perennials and can be over-wintered in the window box.

MATERIALS

60 cm (24 in) stone window box
Crocks or other suitable drainage
* material*
Compost
Slow-release plant food granules

PLANTS

Sedum *'Ruby Glow'*
Marjoram
Lemon thyme (Thymus
  citriodorus)
Common thyme (Thymus
  vulgaris)
Origanum

LEMON
THYME

ORIGANUM

MARJORAM

COMMON
THYME

SEDUM

GARDENER'S TIP

You can imitate the look of an old stone window box by painting a new one with a dilute mixture of liquid seaweed plant food and water. This encourages moss to grow and ages the stone.

PLANT IN SPRING

1 Cover the base of the window box with a layer of crocks or other suitable drainage material. Fill with compost, mixing in 3 teaspoons of slow-release plant food granules.

2 Plant the sedum off-centre to the left of the window box and the marjoram to the left of the sedum.

3 Plant the lemon thyme in the centre front and the common thyme in the back right-hand corner of the container.

4 Plant the origanum in the front right-hand corner of the window box. Water well and place in a sunny position.

Star-jasmine in a Villandry Planter

The soft, seductive scent of the star-jasmine makes this a perfect container to place by the side of a door where the scent will be appreciated by all who pass through.

STAR-
JASMINE

MATERIALS

50 cm (20 in) villandry planter or similar, preferably self-watering
Equal mix loam-based compost and standard compost
Slow-release plant food granules
Bark chippings

PLANTS

Star-jasmine (Trachelospermum jasminoides)

GARDENER'S TIP

Use a plastic liner inside all large planters. It is easier to remove the liner when replanting rather than dismantle the entire container.

PLANT IN LATE SPRING OR EARLY SUMMER

1 Feed the wicks through the holes in the base of the liner.

2 Fill the water reservoir in the base of the planter to the top of the overflow pipe, and place the liner inside the planter.

3 Fill the bottom of the liner with compost while pulling through the wicks so that they reach the level of the roots.

4 Remove the jasmine from its pot, gently tease the roots loose and stand it in the planter.

NOTE *Steps 1–3 are for self-watering planters only.*

5 Add compost and firm it around the rootball of the jasmine. Scatter 2 tablespoons of plant food granules on the surface, and gently work them into the top layer of compost with the trowel.

6 Mulch around the plant with a layer of bark chippings, then water. Check the reservoir of the self-watering container once a week and top up if necessary. Conventional pots should be watered daily in the early morning or evening during hot weather.

Difficult Situations

A shady pathway or a bare corner of the patio may cry out for plants to enliven it,
but it can be hard to know what to grow there. The areas near the house
walls are usually very dry, and may be in shade for most of the day. On the other hand,
paved areas can be so hot and sunny that many plants would not be able to
survive without scorching. Here are some solutions to furnishing the more difficult parts
of the garden. With imaginative use of dramatic foliage and careful
choice of shade-tolerant flowering plants, you can light up the darkest areas
with exciting and colourful arrangements. It really is possible to achieve a flower-filled
hanging basket on a north-facing wall. For windy corners, choose varieties with
wiry stems, such as bidens, that will not suffer from being blown about, and for hot
spots go for sun-lovers like osteospermum or mesembryanthemum.

ABOVE: *Ferns thrive in shady spots and can add a burst of colour to even*
the darkest corner of the garden.

Busy Lizzies in Bloom

There are not many shade-loving plants as colourful and prolific as the busy Lizzie. These plants will very happily bloom all summer long in a hanging basket on a north-facing wall, or in any shady or partially shaded position.

MATERIALS

30 cm (12 in) hanging basket
Sphagnum moss
Compost
Slow-release plant food granules

PLANTS

6 rose-pink lobelias
3 pale pink busy Lizzies
(impatiens)
3 white busy Lizzies
3 dark pink busy Lizzies

LOBELIA

BUSY LIZZIES

1 Line the lower half of the basket with moss and plant three lobelias through the side of the basket near the bottom.

2 Carefully feed the foliage through the sides of the basket. Line the basket with some more moss.

3 Plant one busy Lizzie of each colour. Line the rest of the basket with moss and partly fill with compost, mixing in a teaspoon of plant food granules. Plant the remaining three lobelias into the side of the basket near the top edge. Add more compost.

4 Plant the remaining busy Lizzies in the top of the basket. Water thoroughly and hang in partial or full shade.

GARDENER'S TIP

In wet or windy weather, busy Lizzies can look a bit battered, but once the weather improves, five minutes spent removing dead or damaged flowers will soon restore the basket to its former glory.

PLANT IN LATE SPRING OR EARLY SUMMER

Shady Characters

All the plants used in this window box are perfectly happy in the shade. A periwinkle with variegated leaves and blue spring flowers is planted with blue-leaved hostas and summer-flowering busy Lizzies in a window box that will brighten a gloomy corner for many months.

MATERIALS

45 cm (18 in) fibre window box
Crocks or other suitable drainage material
Compost
Slow-release plant food granules

PLANTS

Variegated periwinkle (Vinca minor 'Aureovariegata')
3 Hosta 'Blue Moon'
5 white busy Lizzies (impatiens)

HOSTA

BUSY LIZZIE

PERIWINKLE

1 Cover the base of the window box with a layer of drainage material. Fill the window box with compost, mixing in 2 teaspoons of slow-release plant food granules.

2 Plant the periwinkle in the centre of the window box.

3 Plant two of the hostas in the back corners of the window box and the third in front of, or slightly to one side of, the periwinkle.

4 Plant the busy Lizzies in the remaining spaces.

GARDENER'S TIP

To keep the busy Lizzies looking their best, pick off the dead flowers and leaves regularly or they will stick to the plant and spoil its appearance.

PLANT IN LATE SPRING

Full of Ferns

A damp shady corner is the perfect position for a basket of ferns. Provided they are regularly fed and watered, and the ferns are cut back in late autumn, this basket will give pleasure for many years. These are hardy ferns, but the idea can be adapted for a conservatory or bathroom using less hardy plants such as the maidenhair fern.

MATERIALS

36 cm (14 in) hanging basket
Sphagnum moss
Compost
Slow-release plant food granules

PLANTS

4 different ferns (dryopteris,
athyrium, Matteuccia
struthiopteris *and* Asplenium
scolopendrium *'Crispum')*

FERNS

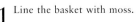

1 Line the basket with moss.

2 Fill the basket with compost. Mix a teaspoon of slow-release plant food granules into the top of the compost.

3 Before removing the ferns from their pots, arrange them in the basket to ensure that you achieve a balanced effect. Plant the ferns and water well.

GARDENER'S TIP

Strange as it may seem, finely chopped banana skins are a favourite food of ferns. Simply sprinkle around the base of the stems and watch the ferns flourish.

PLANT IN SPRING

Bronze and Gold Winners

Bronze pansies and mimulus and golden green lysimachias take the medals in this striking arrangement, with richly coloured heuchera adding to the unusual mixture of tones. This arrangement will work most successfully in a partially shaded situation.

MATERIALS

40 cm (16 in) hanging basket
Sphagnum moss
Compost
Slow-release plant food granules

PLANTS

Heuchera *'Bressingham Bronze'*
3 bronze-coloured pansies (viola)
3 bronze-coloured mimulus
3 Lysimachia nummularia 'Aurea'

LYSIMACHIA

MIMULUS

PANSY

HEUCHERA

1 Line the basket with moss.

2 Fill the basket with compost, mixing a teaspoon of plant food granules into the top layer of compost.

3 Plant the heuchera in the middle of the basket.

4 Plant the pansies, evenly spaced around the heuchera.

5 Plant the three mimulus between the pansies.

6 Plant the lysimachias around the edge of the basket. Water well and hang in light shade.

GARDENER'S TIP

At the end of the season the heuchera can be planted in the border or in another container. It will do best in partial shade, as full sun tends to scorch and discolour the leaves.

PLANT IN SPRING

Shady Corner

Shady corners are often thought of as problematical, when in fact there is a wealth of wonderful plants that thrive in these situations, such as the hosta, hydrangea and fern used in this arrangement.

MATERIALS

3 terracotta pots of various sizes
Crocks or other suitable drainage
* material*
Composted manure
Equal mix standard compost and
* loam-based compost*

PLANTS

Hosta sieboldiana elegans
Variegated hydrangea
Polystichum fern

HYDRANGEA

POLYSTICHUM

HOSTA

GARDENER'S TIP

The hosta is a beautiful foliage plant much loved by slugs and snails which chew unsightly holes in the leaves. To prevent this, smear a broad band of petroleum jelly below the rim of the container and the leaves will remain untouched.

PLANT AT ANY TIME
OF THE YEAR

1 Plant the hosta in a pot large enough for its bulky root system, and with space for further growth. The pot used here nicely echoes the shape of the leaves. Place crocks at the bottom of the pot and then put in a layer of manure before adding the potting compost. Follow this procedure with the hydrangea as well.

2 Plant the fern in a terracotta pot slightly larger than its existing pot. It should not need transplanting for 2–3 years.

3 The hydrangea makes a great deal of growth during the summer and could get very top-heavy. Plant in a sturdy pot with plenty of space for root growth.

A Space in the Sun

Since osteospermum, portulaca and diascia are all sun-lovers this is definitely a basket for your sunniest spot, where the plants will thrive and the colours will look their best.

MATERIALS

36 cm (14 in) hanging basket
Sphagnum moss
Compost
Slow-release plant food granules

PLANTS

6 peach portulaca
Osteospermum 'Buttermilk'
3 Diascia 'Salmon Supreme', or
   similar

PORTULACA

DIASCIA

OSTEOSPERMUM

1 Line the lower half of the basket with moss. Plant three portulaca by resting the rootballs on the moss, and guiding the foliage between the wires.

2 Add more moss to the basket, tucking it carefully around the portulaca.

3 Partly fill the basket with compost, mixing a teaspoon of slow-release plant food granules into the top layer. Plant the remaining three portulaca just below the rim of the basket.

4 Line the rest of the basket with moss. Plant the osteopermum centrally. Plant the diascias around the osteospermum. Water thoroughly and hang in a sunny spot.

GARDENER'S TIP

Keep pinching out the growing tips of the osteospermum to ensure a bushy plant.

PLANT IN LATE SPRING OR
EARLY SUMMER

A Dazzling Display

The succulents in this window box will provide a vivid splash of colour throughout the summer, and will cope very well on a hot dry window-sill. Mesembryanthemum, kalanchoe and portulaca all love the sunshine and will grow happily in this small window box.

PORTULACA

MESEMBRYANTHEMUMS

MATERIALS

36 cm (14 in) plastic window
* box*
Compost
Slow-release plant
* food granules*

PLANTS

Kalanchoe
2 portulaca
3 mesembryanthemum

KALANCHOE

1 Check the drainage holes are open in the base and, if not, drill or punch them open. Fill the window box with compost, mixing in a teaspoon of slow-release plant food granules.

2 Plant the kalanchoe in the centre of the window box.

3 Plant the two portulaca in the front corners of the window box.

4 Plant one mesembryanthemum in front of the kalanchoe and the other two behind the two portulaca. Water well and stand in a sunny position.

GARDENER'S TIP

Since mesembryanthemum flowers open in response to direct sunlight, it is essential to place them in a position where they are in full sun for as long as possible every day.

PLANT IN LATE SPRING OR EARLY SUMMER

Desert Belles

An attractively weathered window box is the container used for this dramatic collection of succulents. With their architectural leaf shapes and wonderful range of colouring they would look particularly good in a modern setting.

MATERIALS

40 cm (16 in) terracotta window box
Crocks or other suitable drainage material
Compost
Gravel
Slow-release plant food granules

PLANTS

Aloe
Crassula ovata
Echeveria elegans
Sansevieria trifasciata

ECHEVERIA

CRASSULA

SANSEVIERIA

ALOE

GARDENER'S TIP

Move the window box to a conservatory or frost-free greenhouse for the winter. Water sparingly only if plants show signs of shrivelling.

PLANT IN LATE SPRING OR EARLY SUMMER FOR OUTDOOR USE, OR ANY TIME OF YEAR FOR A CONSERVATORY

1 Place a layer of crocks or other suitable drainage material in the base of the container. Fill with compost, mixing in a teaspoon of slow-release plant food granules. Plant the aloe at the right-hand end of the window box.

2 Plant the crassula next to the aloe, the echeveria towards the back of the window box, and the sansevieria in front of the echeveria.

3 Surround the plants with a layer of gravel. Water well to establish and thereafter water sparingly. Place in full sun.

Inspirational
Containers

Sometimes a container is so characterful it dictates its own planting scheme.
A wooden tub with an oriental feel, for example, is a perfect container for a delicate
Japanese maple – a restrained yet stunning combination. Or the shape of the
pot may echo that of the flowers, such as lilies planted in a curvaceous urn. Old wooden
boxes and trugs call for cottage-garden mixtures to enhance their old-fashioned
charm. If you can find striking and original containers like these, seek out plants that
suit them and show them to their best advantage.

There are also ideas here for truly dramatic effects; a plunging cascade of
variegated foliage, a black-and-white pot with black and white flowers to match, ivy
trained into a formal topiary shape and a fountain of fuchsias.

ABOVE: *Ivy trained around a shaped hoop adds height and interest to*
this pot of petunias.

Old Favourites

Dianthus, violas and candytuft are delightful cottage-garden plants that make a pretty display during late spring and early summer. Although by the time we took our photograph the candytuft was over, the other flowers were still putting on a good show.

MATERIALS

40 cm (16 in) painted wooden window box
Crocks or other suitable drainage material
Compost
Slow-release plant food granules

PLANTS

Dianthus
Candytuft (iberis)
2 violas

DIANTHUS

CANDYTUFT

VIOLAS

GARDENER'S TIP

Once the flowers are over, cut back the plants and plant them out in the garden. There is still time to replant the window box with summer plants.

PLANT IN EARLY SPRING

1 Cover the base of the container with a layer of drainage material. Fill with compost, mixing in a teaspoon of slow-release plant food granules.

2 Plant the dianthus slightly to the right of the centre of the window box.

3 Plant the candytuft to the left of the centre of the window box beside the dianthus.

4 Plant a viola at each end. Water well and stand in a mixture of sun and shade.

Colourful Evergreens

Evergreen cordyline with its dramatic red spear-shaped leaves, a green hebe and a golden conifer have been mixed with blue-green hostas in a permanent planting, which is given seasonal interest by the addition of red-flowered New Guinea impatiens.

MATERIALS

76 cm (30 in) plastic window box
Compost
Slow-release plant food granules

PLANTS

Red cordyline
Golden conifer Chamaecyparis pisifera
 'Sungold'
Hebe *'Emerald Green'*
Hosta *'Blue Moon'*
Golden grass Hakonechloa 'Aureola'
2 red-flowered New Guinea impatiens

CORDYLINE

HOSTA

IMPATIENS   HEBE

CONIFER

GOLDEN GRASS

GARDENER'S TIP

At the end of the summer replace the impatiens with pansies, polyanthus or heathers.

PLANT IN SPRING

1 Check the drainage holes are open in the base and, if not, drill or punch them open. Fill the window box with compost, mixing in 3 teaspoons of slow-release plant food granules. Plant the cordyline left of centre and the conifer at the right-hand end.

2 Plant the hebe in the centre of the window box. Plant the hosta between the hebe and the conifer.

3 Plant the golden grass at the left-hand end of the window box. Plant the impatiens between the golden grass and the cordyline, and next to the hosta. Water well and stand in partial sun.

A Trough of Alpines

A selection of easy-to-grow alpine plants is grouped in a basket-weave stone planter to create a miniature garden. The mulch of gravel is both attractive and practical as it prevents soil splashing on to the leaves of the plants.

MATERIALS

40 cm (16 in) stone trough
Crocks
Compost
Slow-release plant food granules
Gravel

PLANTS

Sempervivum
Alpine aquilegia
White rock rose (helianthemum)
Papaver alpinum
Alpine phlox
Pink saxifrage
White saxifrage

PAPAVER
ALPINUM

SEMPERVIVUM

SAXIFRAGES

ALPINE PHLOX

ROCK ROSE

ALPINE AQUILEGIA

1 Cover the base of the trough with a layer of crocks. Fill the container with compost, mixing in a teaspoon of slow-release plant food granules and extra gravel for improved drainage.

2 Arrange the plants, still in their pots, in the trough to decide on the most attractive arrangement. Complete the planting, working across the trough.

3 Scatter a good layer of gravel around the plants. Water thoroughly and stand in a sunny position.

GARDENER'S TIP

Tidy the trough once a month, removing dead flowerheads and leaves, adding more gravel if necessary. A trough like this will last a number of years before it needs replanting.

PLANT IN SPRING

The Apothecary's Box

Many plants have healing qualities and, while they should always be used with caution, some of the more commonly used herbs have been successful country remedies for centuries.

CHAMOMILE

FENNEL

MATERIALS

Wooden trug
Crocks or other suitable drainage
  material
Compost
Pelleted chicken manure

MARIGOLD

LAVENDER

ROSEMARY

PLANTS

Lavender – for relaxation
Rosemary – for healthy hair
  and scalp
Chamomile – for restful sleep
Fennel – for digestion
Feverfew – for migraine
3 pot marigolds (calendula) –
  for healing

FEVERFEW

1 Place drainage material in the trug and fill with compost, mixing in 2 teaspoons of fertilizer. Plant a central lavender.

2 Plant the rosemary in the front right-hand corner of the trug.

3 Plant the chamomile in the back left-hand corner.

4 Plant the fennel in the back right-hand corner.

5 Plant the feverfew in the front left-hand corner.

6 Plant the marigolds in the remaining spaces. Water well and stand in full or partial sun.

GARDENER'S TIP

Herbs should not be used to treat any medical condition
without first checking with your medical practitioner.

PLANT IN THE SPRING

Daring Reds and Bold Purples

The colour of the fuschia's flowers is echoed by the deep purple and crimson petunias. The stark white window box provides the perfect contrast to make a bold display.

GARDENER'S TIP

At the end of the season the catmint plants can be trimmed back and planted in the garden. The fuchsia and campanulas can be cut back and potted up to be overwintered in a frost-free greenhouse.

PLANT IN SPRING

MATERIALS

76 cm (30 in) plastic window box
90 cm (3 ft) wooden window box (optional)
Compost
Slow-release plant food granules

PLANTS

Fuchsia 'Dollar Princess'
2 low-growing catmint (Nepeta mussinii)
2 white-flowered Campanula isophylla
2 crimson petunias
2 purple petunias

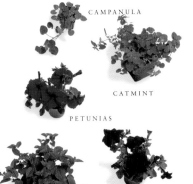
CAMPANULA

CATMINT

PETUNIAS

FUCHSIA

1 Check the drainage holes are open in the base and, if not, drill or punch them open. Fill the window box with compost, mixing in 3 teaspoons of slow-release plant food granules. Plant the fuchsia in the centre.

2 Plant a catmint at each end of the window box. Plant the campanulas next to the catmint.

3 Plant the crimson petunias on either side of the fuchsia at the back and the purple one in front.

4 Water thoroughly and allow to drain. Lower the plastic window box into place inside the wooden window box, if using. Stand in a sunny position.

Chinese Water Garden

In China, glazed pots are frequently used as small ponds in courtyards.
This pot contains a water lily, a flowering rush and an arum lily.

MATERIALS

Water lily basket
Piece of hessian
Aquatic compost
Large bucket
70 cm (28 in) glazed pot
Putty (optional)
Bricks

PLANTS

Compact water lily
  (Nymphaea tetragona)
Flowering rush
  (Butomus umbellatus)
Arum lily (Zantedeschia
  aethiopica)

FLOWERING
RUSH

WATER LILY

ARUM LILY

1 Line the basket with hessian, insert the water lily and top up with aquatic compost. Lower the basket into a bucket of water to settle the compost.

2 If the glazed pot has a drainage hole, plug it with putty and leave to harden overnight. Use bricks to create platforms for the two potted plants.

3 Before filling the pot with water, position the rush so that its pot will be fully submerged and the arum lily so that the pot will be half-submerged.

4 Fill the pot with water and gently lower the water lily into position – its leaves should float on the surface. This water garden will do best in a sunny position.

GARDENER'S TIP

This arrangement is not recommended for anyone with small children; they can drown in a surprisingly small amount of water.

PLANT IN LATE SPRING OR
EARLY SUMMER

Colourful Cooking Pot

Junk shops are a rich source of old pots and pans which can make characterful containers for plants when their kitchen days are over.

PLANTS

Ceratostigma plumbaginoides
Inula *'Oriental Star'*
Golden ivy

CERATOSTIGMA

MATERIALS

30 cm (12 in) cooking pot
Gravel
Equal mix loam-based
   compost and
   container compost
Slow-release plant food granules

IVY

INULA

GARDENER'S TIP

These plants are all perennials. When the ceratostigma and inula have finished flowering, plant them in a border where they will flower again next year.

PLANT IN SPRING OR EARLY SUMMER

1 Make one or two drainage holes in the base of the pot and add a 5 cm (2 in) layer of gravel.

2 Remove the ceratostigma from its pot and plant it at one side of the container.

3 Add the inula and the ivy, and fill in between the plants with compost, firming them in position as you work. Scatter a tablespoon of plant food granules over the surface of the compost. Water and place in a sunny position.

Black-and-White Arrangement

Linking the colour of the container with the plants creates a harmony of design, which is given extra dramatic impact when the colours used are black and white.

MATERIALS

Terracotta pot, 30 cm (12 in) high
Masking tape
Paint brush
Matt white and black paint
Crocks or other suitable
  drainage material
Compost
Slow-release plant food granules
Fine gravel

PLANTS

White osteospermum
Black grass (Ophiopogon planiscapus 'Nigrescens')
3 Viola 'Molly Sanderson'

BLACK
GRASS

VIOLA

OSTEOSPERMUM

1 Mark out a checkered pattern on the pot with masking tape.

2 Paint the top and bottom row of checks white and the rim and the middle row black. Remove the tape.

3 Cover the drainage holes at the bottom of the pot with crocks and half-fill with compost. Plant the osteospermum at the back of the container.

4 Place the black grass next to the osteospermum and top up the container with compost. Plant the three violas in a group.

5 Scatter a tablespoon of plant food granules on the surface of the compost and mulch with fine gravel. Water and stand in a sunny position.

GARDENER'S TIP

Experiment with other colourful themes. You could try a sky blue-and-white check container planted with a morning glory, or a bright red and green pot planted with a red pelargonium.

PLANT IN SPRING OR
EARLY SUMMER

Topiary Ivy with White Petunias

Use wire topiary frames (available at most garden centres) to train ivy or other climbing plants into interesting shapes. The ivy will take some months to establish a strong outline; in the meantime, miniature white petunias complete the picture.

MATERIALS

45 cm (18 in) oval terracotta
  window box
Crocks or other suitable drainage
  material
Compost
Slow-release plant food granules
Wire topiary frame
Pins made from garden wire
Plant rings

PLANTS

2 variegated ivies
4 miniature white petunias

IVIES

PETUNIA

1 Place a layer of drainage material in the base of the window box. Fill the window box with compost, mixing in 2 teaspoons of slow-release plant food granules.

2 Plant the two ivies, one in front of the other in the centre of the window box.

3 Position the topiary frame in the centre of the window box and use pins to hold it in place.

4 Wrap the stems of ivy around the stem of the frame, and then around the frame itself.

5 Cut away any straggly stems and use plant rings to secure the ivy to the frame.

6 Plant the petunias around the topiary ivy. Water thoroughly and stand in light shade.

GARDENER'S TIP

Maintain the shape of the ivy with regular trimming and training – 5 minutes once a week will create a better shape than 15 minutes once a month.

PLANT IVY AT ANY TIME OF YEAR,
PETUNIAS IN SPRING

Dramatic Foliage

GROUND IVY

NEMESIA

BEGONIA

BLACK GRASS

VIOLA

Viola 'Bowles' Black' is combined with black grass – ophiopogon – and the dramatically coloured *Begonia rex*. Pale pink nemesias and variegated ground ivies provide an effective contrast.

MATERIALS

36 cm (14 in) hanging basket
Sphagnum moss
Compost
Slow-release plant food granules

PLANTS

Begonia rex
Black grass (Ophiopogon planiscapus
  'Nigrescens')
2 variegated ground ivies (Glechoma
  hederacea 'Variegata')
2 Nemesia denticulata 'Confetti'
2 Viola 'Bowles' Black'

1 Line the basket with moss and fill it with compost, mixing a teaspoon of plant food granules in the top layer of compost. Plant the begonia at the back of the basket. Plant the black grass in front of the begonia.

2 Plant the ground ivies at either side of the basket, angling the plants so that the foliage tumbles down the sides of the basket.

3 Plant the nemesias on either side of the begonia. Plant the violas on either side of the black grass. Water the basket well and hang in light shade.

GARDENER'S TIP

At the end of the season the begonia can be potted up and kept indoors as a houseplant and the black grass can be planted in an outdoor container.

PLANT IN LATE SPRING OR EARLY SUMMER

Foliage Wall Pot

The bushy growth of *Fuchsia magellanica* 'Alba Variegata' is ideal for displaying as a crown of leafy hair in a head-shaped wall pot. This copy of an ancient Grecian head will add a classical touch to a modern garden.

MATERIALS

Grecian head wall pot
Expanded clay granules

PLANTS

Fuchsia magellanica *'Alba Variegata'*

FUCHSIA

1 Check that the wall pot has a hook or can be hung up. The hanging point will need to be sufficiently strong to carry the weight of a moist pot.

2 Add expanded clay granules to the base of the wall pot to lift the top of the plant to the right level.

3 Place the plant in its pot inside the wall pot.

4 Arrange the foliage to make a convincing leafy crown of hair for the head.

GARDENER'S TIP

Check the base of the pot for drainage holes. If there are no holes, you will need to remove the pot each time you water it, allowing the compost to drain before replacing it.

PLANT AT ANY TIME OF YEAR

Filigree Foliage

The purply-black leaves of this heuchera are all the more stunning when surrounded by the delicate silver-and-green filigree foliage of senecio, the tender *Lavendula pinnata* and the soft lilac-coloured flowers of the bacopa and the brachycome daisies. The plants are grown in a white plastic planter which is concealed inside an elegant wooden window box.

MATERIALS

76 cm (30 in) plastic window box
Compost
Slow-release plant food granules
90 cm (3 ft) wooden window box (optional)

PLANTS

Heuchera *'Palace Purple'*
2 Lavenders
2 blue brachycome daisies
3 Senecio cineraria 'Silver Dust'
2 blue bacopa

SENECIO

LAVENDER

BRACHYCOME

BACOPA

HEUCHERA

1 Check drainage holes are open in the base of the planter and, if not, drill or punch them out. Fill the window box with compost, mixing in 2 teaspoons of slow-release plant food granules. Plant the heuchera in the centre.

2 Plant the two lavenders on either side of the heuchera.

3 Plant the two brachycome daisies at each end of the window box.

4 Place the three senecios at the front of the box between the brachycomes.

5 Plant the two bacopa between the senecio and the heuchera.

6 Water thoroughly and lift into place in the wooden window box, if using. Place in full or partial sun.

GARDENER'S TIP

Wooden window boxes can be assembled so they are self-watering where access is difficult for daily watering. A variety of self-watering containers are available and come with full instructions for their use.

PLANT IN SPRING

Fuchsia Wall Fountain

A dry terracotta wall fountain makes a lovely innovative planting pot. *Fuchsia* 'Daisy Bell' is particularly suited to growing in such a fountain or in a hanging basket. Its growth is trailing, lax and self-branching, and it produces numerous flowers freely throughout the summer.

MATERIALS

Terracotta wall fountain
Bricks
Clay granules
Peat-free compost

PLANTS

3 Fuchsia *'Daisy Bell'*

FUCHSIA

1 Prop the wall fountain securely upright using the bricks. Make sure that the planting bowl is held straight, so that you can create a balanced arrangement.

2 Fill with expanded clay granules and peat-free compost. Add a water-retaining gel if you are concerned about the rapid water-loss from terracotta.

3 Arrange the plants while still in their pots.

4 Plant them when you are satisfied with your arrangement, adding extra compost to cover the rootballs. Finally, add a layer of clay granules to the top of the compost as a mulch to prevent excessive water loss through evaporation.

GARDENER'S TIP

When planting a wall pot, avoid using a fuchsia cultivar that needs regular stopping to encourage branching. Choose a variety like 'Daisy Bell' which is naturally abundant and bushy.

PLANT IN EARLY SPRING OR EARLY SUMMER

Illusions of Grandeur

A small plastic window box takes on unexpected grandeur when filled with rich, velvety purples and pinks, and placed in a stylish setting.

PLANTS

Heliotrope
2 Viola 'Bowles' Black'
Blue verbena
4 lilac lobelias

MATERIALS

30 cm (12 in) plastic window box
Compost
Slow-release plant food granules

GARDENER'S TIP

Dead-head the violas regularly to keep them flowering, and pinch out any straggly stems.

PLANT IN SPRING

HELIOTROPE

VERBENA

LOBELIA

VIOLA

1 Check the drainage holes are open in the base and, if not, drill or punch them open. Fill the container with compost, mixing in a teaspoon of slow-release plant food granules. Plant the heliotrope in the centre at the back.

2 Plant the violas at either end of the window box in the back corners. Plant the verbena centrally in front of the heliotrope.

3 Plant two of the lobelias on either side of the verbena and the others between the heliotrope and the violas. Water thoroughly and stand in partial shade.

Mediterranean Garden

The brilliant colours of the Mediterranean are recreated with these painted pots. While the plants thrive in the climate of the Mediterranean, they also perform perfectly in less predictable weather.

MATERIALS

4 terracotta pots of various sizes
Paint brush
Selection of brightly coloured emulsion paints
Masking tape
Crocks
Loam-based compost with 1/3 added grit
Gravel

PLANTS

Prostrate rosemary
Aloe (optional)
Golden thyme
Large red pelargonium

ROSEMARY

ALOE

PELARGONIUM

1 Paint the pots with solid colours or with patterns using two coats if necessary. The terracotta absorbs the moisture from the paint, so they will dry very quickly.

2 Paint the rim of one pot with a contrasting colour.

3 Create a zig-zag pattern using masking tape and painting alternate sections.

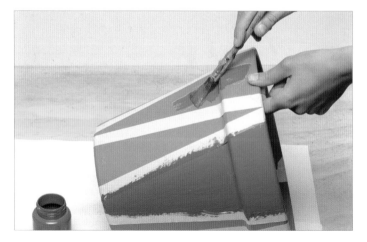

4 Place crocks in the bottom of the pots and then position the plants, firming them in place with extra compost. The compacted roots of this rosemary will benefit from being teased loose before planting.

5 The aloe does not need a large pot. Plant it in a pot just slightly larger than the one you bought it in.

6 Plant the thyme and pelargonium in separate pots. Finish the plants with a top-dressing of gravel, water well and place in a sheltered sunny corner.

GARDENER'S TIP

For commercial reasons the plants you buy will probably have been grown in a peat compost, although they prefer a loam-based compost. Gently loosen the peat around their roots and mix it with the loam-based compost before potting up in the new mixture.

PLANT IN LATE SPRING OR EARLY SUMMER

Japanese-style Planter

A wooden apple barrel makes an inexpensive container for this Japanese maple. The tree is surrounded by moss and stones to create the effect of a Japanese garden. This planted container is designed to be very lightweight and would be ideal for a roof terrace or balcony.

MATERIALS

Apple barrel or similar wooden tub
Plastic saucer to fit the bottom of
* the container*
Slow-release plant food granules
Perlite or polystyrene packing material
Bun moss
Large stones

JAPANESE
MAPLE

PLANT

Japanese maple (Acer palmatum var. dissectum)

GARDENER'S TIP

The tree should be checked annually to see if it needs repotting. If roots are showing through the base of the pot this is a sure sign that the tree should be moved into a larger one. If weight is not a consideration use clay granules instead of perlite or polystyrene.

PLANT AT ANY TIME OF THE YEAR

1 Place the plastic saucer in the base of the container.

2 Stand the tree in its pot in the saucer. Scatter half a tablespoon of slow-release plant food granules on the surface of the compost. Fill the area around the pot with perlite or polystyrene.

3 Cover the surface of the perlite or polystyrene with bun moss interspersed with stones. Place in full or partial sun and water regularly.

Regency Lily Urn

The shape of this urn is based on the shape of the lily flower, so it makes an appropriate container for this lovely mix of lilies, lavenders, pink marguerites and helichrysums.

MATERIALS

Suitably shaped urn
Gravel
Loam-based compost
  with ⅓ added grit
Slow-release plant
  food granules

PLANTS

2 *white lilies*
2 *Lavenders* (Lavandula *'Hidcote')*
2 *pink marguerites* *(argyranthemums)*
3 Helichrysum petiolare

LILY
LAVENDER
MARGUERITE
HELICHRYSUM

1 Place a 5 cm (2 in) layer of gravel at the bottom of the urn and half-fill with compost. Place the lilies in the centre.

2 Arrange the lavenders and marguerites around the lilies.

3 Plant the helichrysums around the edge of the urn so that they cascade over the rim as they grow. Fill between the plants with additional compost enriched with a tablespoon of slow-release plant food granules. Water well and place in a sunny position.

GARDENER'S TIP

Cut back the lavender heads when they have finished flowering, leave the lilies to die down naturally, and dead-head the marguerites regularly to keep them flowering all summer. The helichrysums and marguerites are not frost hardy, but the lavenders and lilies should bloom again next year.

PLANT IN SPRING

Standard Fuchsia

Fuchsia 'Tom West' is an excellent hardy variety which was raised in 1853. Here, underplanted with variegated ivy, and benefiting from the large Chinese-style glazed pot, the display has a very modern chic appeal.

MATERIALS

*Large glazed pot, at least 70 cm
  (28 in) diameter
Crocks
Peat-free compost
Slow-release plant food granules*

PLANTS

1 half-standard Fuchsia *'Tom
  West'
6 variegated ivies*

FUCHSIA

IVY

1 Cover the drainage hole in the base of the pot with the crocks. This prevents it from becoming blocked and facilitates the free drainage of excess water from the compost.

2 Almost fill the pot with peat-free compost. Add slow-release plant food granules to the compost.

3 Remove the half-standard fuchsia from its pot, and lower it gently on to the compost so that the top of its rootball is slightly lower than the lip of the pot.

4 Add more compost. Plant the variegated ivies around the base of the fuchsia. Fill in the gaps between the rootballs, and tease the ivies' stems and foliage across the compost surface. Water to settle the compost.

GARDENER'S TIP

The variegated foliage of 'Tom West' develops a lovely rich pink colouring when grown in a sunny position. The best foliage colour is on the young growth, so regular pinching out of new stem tips will ensure a colourful plant.

PLANT IN EARLY SPRING OR EARLY SUMMER

Galvanized-bath Garden

An old tin bath makes an ideal planter; it is large and deep enough to take quite large plants. Here, foxgloves and euphorbias are underplanted with violets, making an attractive early summer display.

EUPHORBIA

FOXGLOVE

VIOLET

MATERIALS

Tin bath, 60 cm (24 in) wide
Gravel or similar drainage material
Equal mix loam-based compost and
   standard compost
Slow-release plant food granules

PLANTS

3 foxgloves (digitalis)
2 euphorbia
3 violets (viola)

1 If the bath does not have drainage holes, you should make some in the base, and then cover it with a 10 cm (4 in) layer of gravel or similar drainage material. Half-fill the bath with the compost mix, and position the foxgloves.

2 Next add the euphorbia, teasing loose the roots to enable growth if they are at all potbound. Fill between the plants with compost, pressing down firmly around the rootballs.

3 Finally, plant the violets around the edges, where they can tumble over the sides as they grow. Water and place in a shady position.

GARDENER'S TIP

Buy your foxgloves before they have formed their flower spikes; they will transplant better and you will have the pleasure of watching them grow. Do not cut the stems down after flowering; when you can hear the seeds rattling, simply shake them over any corner of the garden where you would like foxgloves to grow.

PLANT IN AUTUMN OR SPRING

Chimney Pot Clematis

It is well known that clematis love to have their heads in the sun and their roots in the shade. A chimney pot creates the perfect environment as it provides exactly these conditions. Ideally, the clematis should be planted in soil with the chimney pot placed over it, but with a little care, pot-grown plants will do well for a few years.

MATERIALS

2 x 20 cm (8 in) plastic pots
Gravel or other suitable drainage
   material
Equal mix loam-based compost
   and container compost
Slow-release plant food granules
60 cm (24 in) chimney pot

PLANTS

Clematis 'Prince
   Charles'

CLEMATIS

1 Fill one of the plastic pots with gravel.

2 Plant the clematis in the other plastic pot, filling around the rootball with the compost mix. Scatter a tablespoon of plant food granules over the surface of the compost. (The two pots will be positioned one on top of the other inside the chimney pot, as shown.)

3 Place the chimney pot over the pot of gravel and then carefully lower the clematis into position. It will need a sunny position and regular watering.

GARDENER'S TIP

Clematis can suffer from clematis wilt: suddenly whole stems will start to wilt and die. Cut all affected growth away from the plant and spray the remaining plant fortnightly with a product containing Benolyl.

PLANT IN SPRING

A Topiary Planting

BOX PYRAMID

BOX BALL

BACOPA

Topiary box plants remain in their pots in this window box. A mulch of bark conceals the pots and retains moisture, and small pots of white bacopa add another dimension to the sculptured design.

MATERIALS

64 cm (25 in) terracotta planter
Bark chippings

PLANTS

Box pyramid in 5 litre (9 in) pot
2 box balls in 5 litre (9 in) pot
5 pots white bacopa

1 Water all the plants thoroughly. Stand the box pyramid in its pot in the centre of the container.

2 Stand the box balls on either side of the pyramid.

3 Fill the container with bark chippings to hide the pots.

4 Plunge the pots of bacopa in the bark at the front of the container. Stand in light shade. Water regularly.

GARDENER'S TIP

Provided the box plants are not root-bound they will be quite happy in their pots for a year. If the leaves start to lose their glossy dark green colour, it is a sign that they need a feed. Sprinkle a long-term plant food on the surface of the pots and boost with a liquid feed.

PLANT BOX AT ANY TIME OF THE YEAR,
AND BACOPA IN SPRING

The Young
Container Gardener

Most children become enthusiastic gardeners as soon as they have a patch of soil they can really call their own, and this applies equally to containers. What is more, if they can make or decorate their container before planting it up, they'll get a real sense of achievement. These projects use easily available plants and seeds that can be bought with pocket money and are reliable and free-flowering, given a little care and attention. There are suggestions for easy-to-grow vegetables and a small pond made from a toy-box that will quickly become a haven for wildlife. Youngsters will have every reason to be proud of the results.

ABOVE: *An old pair of boots can make a fun container for brightly coloured flowers.*

Watering Can Planter

An old watering can makes an attractive container, especially when it is painted and stencilled. When planted with an evergreen plant, such as the ivy used here, it will provide an eye-catching year-round display.

MATERIALS

Old watering can
Paintbrush
Eggshell paint, for the base coat
Stencil design
Masking tape
Stencil brush
Stencil paints, for the decoration
Fine paintbrush
Bark chippings
Slow-release plant food granules

PLANT

Ivy

1 Paint the watering can with the base colour. Apply two coats if necessary and leave each coat to dry thoroughly before painting the next.

2 Fasten the stencil design in place with masking tape. When stencilling, the brush should not hold much paint; dab it on newspaper to get rid of the excess. Use two or three colours to give your design a more three-dimensional effect.

GARDENER'S TIP

Other galvanized tin containers such as tin baths and buckets may also be painted and used.

PLANT AT ANY TIME OF
THE YEAR

3 Use the fine paintbrush to paint the rim of the can. You could pick out additional detailing if you wish.

4 When all the paint is quite dry, fill the watering can with bark chippings.

5 Scoop out a hollow in the chippings and plant the ivy in its pot. Scatter some slow-release plant food granules on the surface. Arrange the tendrils so that they trail over the handle and spout of the watering can. Water, pouring any excess water out through the spout. Place the watering can in a shady spot or hang it from a hook in a cool corner.

Seaside Garden

Even if you live miles from the sea you can create your own garden in
a sunny corner with some seashells, succulents and driftwood.

LAMPRANTHUS

MATERIALS

Seashells
Self-hardening clay
4 terracotta pots of various sizes
Loam-based compost with
 ⅓ added grit
Gravel
Driftwood

PLANTS

Gazania
3 mesembryanthemum
2 crassula
Upright lampranthus
2 trailing lampranthus

GAZANIA

1 Fill the shells with clay,
leaving some unfilled to cover
the compost.

2 Press the shells onto the
terracotta pots and leave the
clay to harden overnight.

3 Plant the gazania in one of the
larger pots.

4 Plant the three
mesembryanthemums as a
group in one pot.

5 Plant the crassulas together in
a fairly small pot. These plants
grow naturally in poor soils and
do not mind overcrowding.

6 The upright and trailing
lampranthus have similar
colour foliage and flower but quite
different shapes so they make an
interesting contrast when planted
together. Cover the compost in
each pot with a layer of gravel and
then add seashells and pieces of
driftwood. Group together in a
sunny position.

Small is Beautiful

Not everyone has room for a large hanging basket, especially when the plants have reached maturity, but there is sure to be space for a small basket like this one which will flower cheerfully all summer long.

MATERIALS

25 cm (10 in) hanging basket
Sphagnum moss
Compost
Slow-release plant food granules

PLANTS

4 nasturtiums
2 Lysimachia nummularia 'Aurea'
3 pot marigolds (calendula)

NASTURTIUM

LYSIMACHIA

MARIGOLDS

GARDENER'S TIP

Small baskets dry out very quickly so be sure to water frequently. To give a really good soak you can immerse the basket in a bucket of water, but be careful not to damage the trailing plants.

PLANT IN SPRING

1 Line the lower half of the basket with moss. Plant three of the nasturtiums into the side of the basket by resting the rootballs on the moss and carefully guiding the leaves through the sides of the basket.

2 Line the rest of the basket with moss and fill with compost, mixing half a teaspoon of slow-release plant food granules into the top layer. Plant the lysimachia opposite one another at the edge of the basket.

3 Plant the pot marigolds in the top of the basket.

4 Plant the remaining nasturtium in the middle of the basket. Water well and hang in a sunny postion.

Terrific Tyres

Old car tyres get a new and completely different lease of life with a lick of paint. They make perfect containers for all sorts of plants and are ideal for a first garden.

BEDDING PLANTS

MATERIALS

Coloured emulsion paints
Paintbrush
2 car tyres
Compost and garden soil
Newspaper

PLANTS

Selection of bedding plants
such as cosmea
pelargoniums, pansies
(viola), and pot marigolds
(calendula)

1 Use ordinary emulsion to paint the tyres – any colours look good, the brighter the better.

2 Put one tyre on top of another and fill with potting compost or equal quantities of garden soil and compost. To cut down on the amount of compost, stuff newspaper into the tyres.

3 Put the tallest plants in first – this is a cosmea. Surround it with smaller plants like pelargoniums, pansies and marigolds.

4 Plant some delicate trailing plants to grow over the edge. Start your tyre garden off by giving it a lot of water. Keep watering through the summer and do not let it get too dry.

GARDENER'S TIP

You can get old tyres for free at most garages. For something cheap and fast-growing, try growing pumpkin plants. A ring of lobelia will grow happily if planted between two tyres.

Blooming Old Boots

This is a blooming wonderful way to recycle an old pair of boots, the bigger the better. It just goes to show that almost anything can be used to grow plants in, as long as it has a few holes in the bottom for drainage. Try an old football, a sports bag, or even an old hat for plant containers with lots of character.

BEDDING PLANTS

MATERIALS

Knife
Old pair of working boots
Compost

PLANTS

Selection of bedding plants such as impatiens, pelargoniums, verbenas, pansies and lobelias

1 Using a knife very carefully, make some holes in between the stitching of the sole for drainage. It helps if there are holes there already.

2 Fill the boots with compost, pushing it down right to the toe so there are no air spaces.

3 Plant flowers like pelargoniums, that can cope with hot dry places, and verbenas which will trail over the edge.

4 Squeeze in a pansy with a contrasting flower colour and a trailing lobelia plant. Lobelia grows in the smallest of spaces and will delicately tumble over the edge.

5 The boots need watering every day in the summer, and bloom even better if some plant food is mixed into the water once a week.

SAFETY NOTE

Children should always be supervised when using any sharp objects.

PLANT IN SPRING

A Watery World

No garden is complete without the sight and sound of water. Great for toe-dipping on a hot sunny day, this mini-pond is too small for fish but a welcome watering spot for thirsty birds. Any large container can be used to make a mini-pond, as long as it is watertight. A toy-tidy, like this one, is ideal.

MATERIALS

Large, wide container
Gravel
Lead from a wine bottle top
Flower pot

PLANTS

2 aquatic plants such as golden sedge and monkey flower
Strands of oxygenating weed
Small floating plants such as water lettuce and floating ferns

1 Put a layer of gravel in the bottom of a large, wide container and fill with water almost to the top.

2 Lower the aquatic plants (which should be in net pots when you buy them) gently into the water around the edge.

3 Bend a piece of lead around the base of pieces of oxygenating weed to weigh them down. Pot the bunch into a flower pot and put a layer of gravel on the surface.

4 Lower the pot into the mini-pond, then add a few floating plants. Sink the pond into a hole in the garden so that it keeps cool.

AQUATIC PLANTS

FLOATING PLANTS

OXYGENATING WEED

GARDENER'S TIP

Keep shallow containers in a semi-shady area to avoid excess evaporation. Plant up an adjoining mix of tulips and alliums for a spring and early summer display.

PLANT IN SPRING

Good Enough to Eat!

You do not need a large garden to grow fruit and vegetables – it is possible to grow some in just a window box. Strawberries and bush or trailing tomatoes are small enough, so are radishes and lettuces. Nasturtium leaves and flowers are edible, with a hot, peppery taste. They look lovely in a salad.

MATERIALS

76 cm (30 in) plastic window box
Compost

PLANTS

2 tomato plants
2 strawberry plants
Radish seeds
Lettuce seeds
Nasturtium seeds

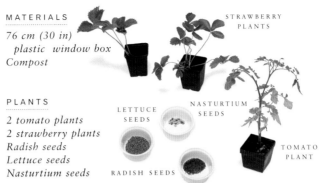

STRAWBERRY PLANTS

LETTUCE SEEDS

NASTURTIUM SEEDS

TOMATO PLANT

RADISH SEEDS

1 Fill the window box with compost to just below the rim. Plant the tomatoes in the back corners of the window box.

2 Plant the strawberries, about 30 cm (12 in) away from the tomatoes.

3 Sow radish and lettuce seeds 1 cm (½ in) apart. After the young radishes have been harvested, the lettuces can grow into their space.

4 Sow some nasturtium seeds in the corners so that they can grow up and trail over the edge. Water thoroughly.

GARDENER'S TIP

To get a plant out of a pot, turn it upside down with the stem between your fingers. With the other hand, firmly squeeze the bottom of the pot to release the rootball.

PLANT IN SPRING

Garden with a Buzz

To encourage beautiful butterflies and buzzing bees into the
garden, grow a few of their
favourite plants to tempt them
in from miles around. Many
butterflies are now becoming
scarce, so every butterfly-
friendly plant that you can
grow will help them to survive.
Bees and butterflies like lots
of sunshine so put the barrel or
planter in a sunny spot.

MATERIALS

Pebbles
Large planter or half barrel
Compost or equal quantities of
  garden soil and compost

PLANTS

Selection of suitable plants such
as phlox, aster, lavender,
verbena, blue lobelia, scabious

PLANTS

GARDENER'S TIP

Other excellent plants are broom,
catmint, delphinium, nasturtium,
ox-eye daisy, petunia, primrose,
stock, sweet William and thrift.

PLANT IN SPRING

1 Put a few pebbles in the
bottom of the barrel or planter
for drainage, then fill with
compost or an equal mixture of
soil and compost.

2 Plant phlox and aster in the
middle because they will grow
the tallest.

3 Plant lavender and verbena
around the edge.

4 Plant blue lobelia in the front,
so it tumbles over the edge.
Water the container.

Fuchsias for Tots

Several fuchsia cultivars are excellent plants for children to grow. These fuchsias can be bought at the start of the summer in small pots or in polystyrene trays. Transferred to small, brightly painted pots on a window-sill, or in a light corner in the children's room, they will flower continuously through the summer.

FUCHSIA

MATERIALS

7.5 cm (3 in) terracotta pots
Paintbrush
Bright acrylic or emulsion paints
Crocks
Compost

PLANTS

Fuchsia *'Happy'* and F. *'Tom Thumb'*

1 Paint the pots with bright primary colours in stripes or bold patterns. The paints used here are thick and water-resistant. If you use ordinary emulsion, you may need a couple of coats to achieve a bold effect. To achieve geometric patterns, use masking tape to mask out specific areas before painting. Let the paint dry before you continue.

2 Place small crocks in the bottom of the pots to cover the drainage hole and facilitate quick drainage.

3 Remove the fuchsias from their plastic pots and place one in each terracotta pot. Add more compost down the sides of the pot.

4 Use the blunt end of the paintbrush to ease the compost into the gap between the plant's rootball and the pot. Tamp down the compost firmly but not too tightly. Water the pots and allow to drain.

PLANT IN EARLY SPRING,
OR EARLY SUMMER

Spring into Action

On misty, autumn days spring might seem a long time away, but young gardeners have to think ahead. If you want a cheerful pot of flowers to greet you early next year, now is the time to get planting. There are hundreds of different types of spring-flowering bulbs to choose from, and mixed and matched with forget-me-nots, daisies, pansies or wallflowers, you cannot go wrong.

MATERIALS

Large flower pot
Small stones
Compost

PLANTS

Tulip bulbs
Wallflowers
  (cheiranthus)
Forget-me-nots,
  daisies or
  pansies (violas)

FORGET-ME-NOT

TULIP BULBS

WALLFLOWERS

GARDENER'S TIP

The plants will not need heavy watering over the autumn and winter, but they will need an occasional drink so keep an eye on the pot in case it dries out.

PLANT IN AUTUMN

1 Use the biggest pot that you have got and put a few stones over the hole in the bottom for drainage. Fill the pot two-thirds full with compost.

2 Plant about 5 tulip bulbs. Cover the bulbs with handfuls of compost.

3 Using your hands to make holes, plant three wallflowers evenly spaced out. If you dig up a tulip bulb by mistake, just pop it back in again.

4 Fill any gaps with forget-me-nots, daisies or pansies, or a mixture. Give all the plants a good watering.

Cactus Garden

Planting a bowl of cacti may take a little care and patience, but it is worth the effort since children love cacti. Once planted, the cacti ask nothing more than benevolent neglect.

MATERIALS

25 cm (10 in) terracotta bowl
Cactus compost
Newspaper
Cactus gravel

PLANTS

Euphorbia submammilaris
Rebutia muscula
*Rose pincushion (*Mammilaria zeilmanniana)
Cheiridopsis candidissima
Astrophytum ornatum
Prickly pear (Opuntia)

REBUTIA   EUPHORBIA   PRICKLY PEAR

CHEIRIDOPSIS

ASTROPHYTUM

ROSE PINCUSHION

GARDENER'S TIP

If there are young children in your household be sure to choose the site of your cactus garden with care. If cacti are too aggressive for you, plant succulents instead: they require the same treatment, but are free of thorns.

PLANT AT ANY TIME
OF THE YEAR

1 Fill the bowl with cactus compost to within 5 cm (2 in) of the rim. Prepare a thickly folded strip of newspaper to help you handle the cacti.

2 Before planting, decide on your arrangement of the plants by standing them, in their pots, in the bowl.

3 Ease the plants from their pots, surround them with a newspaper collar and lift into place. Handle more ferocious plants carefully, and leave the really prickly cacti until last or you will stab yourself on them as you are planting the rest.

4 Fill in around the plants with extra compost if needed. Add a finishing touch with a top-dressing of fine cactus gravel. Stand in good light and water sparingly.

Indoor Containers

Plants do furnish a room, and the same considerations apply to the effective use of containers indoors as in the garden: find containers that suit their surroundings and the plants you have chosen for them; plant them imaginatively and group them for impact. Foliage plants will form the backbone of most arrangements, rather as trees and shrubs do in the garden. Flowering plants won't be so long-lasting indoors, but are always the centre of attraction while they are in bloom.

Decorative pots intended to go outdoors can be used very successfully indoors too. Baskets make good plant holders if you line them with plastic. Your indoor plants will appreciate good light (although direct sunlight through glass is too powerful for most species) and a moist atmosphere: stand the pots in saucers of wet gravel and give them a daily misting to help keep them looking their best.

ABOVE: *Introduce flowering plants to your indoor collections to brighten up your home.*

Indoor Table-top Garden

Many indoor plants have dramatically coloured flowers and foliage. In this arrangement the purple flowers of the African violet are echoed by the velvety leaves of the gynura. The delicate fronds of the maidenhair fern and the dark green foliage of the button fern add interest with their contrasting shape and colour.

MATERIALS

30 cm (12 in) terracotta seed
 tray
Crocks
Houseplant compost
Slow-release plant food granules
Clay granules

PLANTS

Maidenhair fern (adiantum)
African violet (saintpaulia)
Gynura
Button fern (Pellaea rotundifolia)

AFRICAN VIOLET

MAIDENHAIR
FERN

GARDENER'S TIP

Terracotta transmits moisture and will mark a table-top if it is in direct contact with it. Cut 2.5 cm (1 in) sections from a cork and glue them to the four corners of the seed tray. A plastic tray smaller than the seed tray can then be slipped underneath it to catch any drips.

PLANT AT ANY TIME
OF THE YEAR

1 Cover the drainage holes in the bottom of the seed tray with crocks.

2 Arrange the plants before removing them from their pots. Plant the tallest plant first, then add the others around it.

3 Fill any gaps with compost and scatter a tablespoon of plant food granules on the surface. Mulch between the plants with clay granules to help retain moisture. Water and place in a light position, but out of direct sunlight. Spray regularly with water.

Bottle it Up

Bottle gardens are great fun to make, and if you choose a stoppered bottle you will probably be able to grow some of those tricky plants that demand very high humidity. Don't worry too much about choosing the right plants, however. If you are prepared to replace plants when they outgrow their space, just concentrate on the plants that please you. You will have to improvise tools for your bottle garden by lashing old pieces of cutlery to garden canes.

SMALL FOLIAGE PLANTS

MATERIALS

Large glass bottle with cork
Fine gravel
Paper or thin cardboard
Charcoal
Compost
Knife, fork, spoon and
  cotton reel attached to canes

PLANTS

Small foliage plants

1 Place some fine gravel in the bottom of the bottle. If the neck is narrow you can make yourself a funnel from paper or thin cardboard to scatter it evenly over the base.

2 Add a thin layer of charcoal. This will help to absorb impurities and reduce the risk of the bottle smelling if there is too much moisture.

3 Spread a layer of compost over the base, and level it. Using your improvised trowel, make a hole for the plant.

4 Firm each plant in well. If you can't reach with your hand, use a cotton reel pushed on to the end of a cane to tamp down the compost.

5 Work around the whole bottle until it is fully planted. Then mist the plants. Aim the spray at the sides of the bottle if compost is clinging to the glass and spoiling the effect. Leave the plants and compost moist but not soaking wet.

6 If using a stoppered bottle you will have to balance the atmosphere over a week or two. You may need to keep inserting or removing the cork for periods (see opposite).

GARDENER'S TIP

Place the cork firmly in position and leave it for a day or two. Some misting of the glass, especially in the morning,
is quite normal – but if it never clears there is too much moisture, so leave the cork off for a day and try again.
If no condensation appears at all, it is probably too dry – mist again, then return the cork. It will take trial and error at
first, but once the atmosphere is balanced you can leave the bottle for months without attention, although you will have
to prune or remove plants that become too large.

PLANT IN SPRING

Palm Court

Palms look graceful and elegant. They usually look best in isolation or among other palms, rather than in a group of mixed plants. Display them so that their classic shape can be appreciated. Allow these aristocrats space to make a statement.

MATERIALS

Decorative pot with drainage hole
Polystyrene or other suitable drainage material
Compost (loam-based if the plant is large)
Bark chippings

PLANT

Palm, appropriate for size of pot

PALM

1 Unless your palm is small (a few never grow large in the home), choose a large pot. As it will be conspicuous, choose an attractive, decorative one that does the plant justice. Start by placing a layer of polystyrene or other drainage material in the bottom.

2 Stand the palm in the pot and surround the rootball with container compost, pressing it firmly around the plant. Scatter a tablespoon of plant food granules on the surface.

3 Cover the compost with a layer of bark and water. Place in a position that receives good light, but no more than a couple of hours of direct sunlight each day. Water regularly during growing season, but allow the compost to dry out between waterings during the winter.

GARDENER'S TIP

Palms can look splendid in isolation, but they usually look more impressive in a collection. Display plants of different sizes to add interest, and place small ones on pedestals in front of taller ones in large pots. Like most houseplants, the palm will benefit from being stood outside during warm summer rain. A good soaking shower removes dust from the leaves and gives the plant the benefit of a drink of untreated water.

PLANT IN SPRING

Colourful Kitchen Herbs

Make a bright cheerful statement by
using painted tins as containers
for your kitchen herbs, often now
available in pots
from most
supermarkets.

PARSLEY   CORIANDER

BASIL

MATERIALS	PLANTS
Empty food tins	*Dill*
White spirit	*Chives*
Masking tape	*Parsley*
Paintbrush	*Coriander*
Gloss paint	*Basil*

GARDENER'S TIP

Large painted tins make colourful planters in the garden.
Ask your local restaurant or school for some of the catering size tins that
they normally throw away.

PLANT AT ANY TIME OF THE YEAR

1 Thoroughly wash and dry the
tins. Use white spirit to
remove any residual spots of glue.
Wrap masking tape round the lips
of the tins so that half of it
protrudes above the rims.

2 Fold the protruding masking
tape inside the rims of the tins.

3 Paint the tins and leave them
to dry.

4 Depending on the colours you
choose, some of them may
need more than one coat. Leave to
dry completely.

5 Place each plant, pot and all,
in a separate tin. Stand in a
light position and water if the
compost dries out.

Sweet Scents for a Conservatory

This simple, very informal planting would thrive in a conservatory. A pretty combination of scented-leaf pelargonium, deep blue miniature petunias, purple trailing verbenas and exuberant tumbling ground ivies.

VERBENA

GROUND IVY

MATERIALS

30 cm (12 in) plastic window box
Compost
Slow-release plant food granules

PLANTS

Scented-leaf Pelargonium *'Lady Plymouth'*
2 variegated ground ivies (Glechoma hederacea 'Variegata')
2 deep purple trailing verbenas
2 deep blue 'Junior' petunias

PETUNIA

PELARGONIUM

1 Check drainage holes are open; if not, drill or punch them out. Fill the window box with compost, mixing in a teaspoon of slow-release plant foot granules. Plant the pelargonium in the centre.

GARDENER'S TIP

If the ground ivy gets too rampant, cut it back. Root some pieces and plant out in the spring to run wild over a wall.

PLANT IN SPRING

2 Plant the ground ivies at each end, and the two verbenas at the back of the box between the pelargonium and ground ivies.

3 Plant the petunias between the pelargonium and ground ivies at the front of the box. Water thoroughly and stand in a sunny position.

Water-loving Plants

The sweet flag is a marsh plant which loves the moist conditions in most bathrooms. Planted in gravel in a stylish glass pot or vase, it is easy to see when the water needs topping up.

SWEET
FLAG

MATERIALS

20 cm (8 in) glass vase or pot
Gravel

PLANTS

1 large or 2 small sweet flags
(Acorus gramineus 'Variegatus')

1 Fill the bottom half of the container with gravel.

2 Take the plants out of their existing pots and place them on the gravel.

3 Fill the pot with gravel to the base of the leaves and half-fill the container with water. Place on a light window-sill and never allow the plants to dry out.

GARDENER'S TIP

The umbrella plant (Cyperus alternifolius) will also thrive in these conditions.

PLANT AT ANY TIME OF THE YEAR

Combined Effects

Displaying houseplants in groups creates a humid microclimate, which the plants prefer to the dry atmosphere of most homes. The humidity is increased by standing the pots in saucers of wet gravel kept moist by regular watering. Choose plants of contrasting shapes and sizes for the most striking effect.

MATERIALS

4 pots of various sizes with
  saucers
Crocks
Compost
Gravel

PLANTS

Lilies
Maidenhair fern
  (adiantum)
Cretan fern
Variegated creeping fig
  (Ficus pumila)

LILY

MAIDENHAIR
FERN

CREEPING
FIG

CRETAN
FERN

1 Place the crocks in the bottom of the pots. Check the proportion of pot to plant.

2 Remove the lilies from their plastic container and position in the pot.

3 Fill gaps around the rootballs with compost, pressing down firmly to avoid any air spaces.

5 Water the plants thoroughly. Fill the saucers with gravel. Stand the pots in their saucers and position the plants in good light, but away from direct sun. Keep the gravel in the saucers damp, and water the plants when the compost dries out.

4 Remove the foliage plants from their containers and plant in the other pots, topping up with compost.

GARDENER'S TIP

Bear in mind the background of your display when choosing your plants. Large architectural leaves and strong plain colours won't get lost against a busy wallpaper, whereas lots of variegations and colour are better against a plain background.

PLANT AT ANY TIME OF THE YEAR

Beautiful Baskets

A basket is a great way to display a small group of houseplants. You don't need a lot of plants to make a superb show, and when one is past its best you can just remove it and pop in a replacement.

MATERIALS

Basket
Plastic sheet
Compost
Sphagnum moss or
*   fresh moss*

PLANTS

5–6 small plants such as saintpaulia (African violet), chlorophytum, adiantum and exacum, maidenhair fern

CHLOROPHYTUM
MAIDENHAIR
FERN

SAINTPAULIA

ADIANTUM

EXACUM

1 To protect the basket (and your furniture) from the effects of moisture, line it with a piece of plastic cut to size.

2 Add a layer of compost to retain moisture, and provide a humid atmosphere around the plants.

3 Remove the plants from their pots and place in the basket. It may be necessary to remove some compost from the bottom, or add a little more to bring each plant to the right height.

4 Make sure you are entirely happy with the arrangement of the plants, then trickle a little more compost between them to fill in the gaps.

5 Use dried or fresh moss to fill any spaces between the plants.

GARDENER'S TIP

You could leave the plants in the individual pots for convenience.

PLANT AT ANY TIME OF YEAR

Indoor Topiary

Proper topiary is not practical indoors, but you can cheat a little and achieve a similar effect by training ivy over a frame. Start with an easy shape like the lollipop shown here, and once you are proficient you can experiment with all kinds of imaginative shapes. Buy a wire frame or make your own.

MATERIALS

Pot large enough to accommodate frame
Crocks or bark chippings
Compost
Wire frame

PLANTS

IVY

2–3 small-leaved variegated ivies

1 Place crocks or large pieces of bark chippings over the drainage hole and cover with a layer of compost.

2 Insert the wire frame, making sure it is placed centrally, and top up with more compost to secure it.

3 Insert the ivies around the edge of the pot. The more plants you use, the more quickly the frame will be covered.

4 Leave a few shoots to trail over the edge of the pot, but thread the rest through the frame. Within a few months the frame will probably be completely hidden by the new growth. Thread new shoots through bare areas, and pinch back any that are too long. Regular pinching back of long shoots will help to retain the shape once the frame has been covered.

GARDENER'S TIP

Once you have mastered this lollipop shape, try making an animal (teddy bear or rabbit). If you can't find a ready made template, then make your own wire shape. Alternatively, try something more ambitious like a large cup and saucer, or even a tennis racket.

PLANT IN EARLY SPRING

Terrarium Display

FOLIAGE AND
FLOWERING
PLANTS

Terrariums are similar to bottle gardens and come in a variety of shapes. Many of them are not sealed, so the atmosphere is less humid. They provide a more ornamental way to display plants. If access is easy, you may want to consider a few flowering plants to provide colour.

MATERIALS

Terrarium
Expanded clay granules
Gravel
Compost

PLANTS

Selection of small plants

1 Place a layer of expanded clay granules, followed by gravel, in the base to reduce the risk of the compost becoming water-logged. Use either gravel or clay granules if you cannot get both.

2 Add the compost, making the layer several centimetres deep if possible. If this is not practical because of the design of the terrarium, you will need to reduce the depth of the rootballs.

3 If your centrepiece plant is too large, try a little judicious pruning with scissors.

4 You should be able to plant and firm the plants by hand. Plant the back, or the least accessible area first.

5 Place the plants most likely to require regular pruning or pinching back in the most accessible positions.

6 Plant your centrepiece, firming it in well.

GARDENER'S TIP

Be sure that you select slow-growing small-leaved plants, or what began as an airy, well-presented display could end up as a miniature jungle.

PLANT IN EARLY SPRING

Mixed Blessings

A bowl of mixed plants almost always looks better than the same number dotted around in individual pots. Garden centres and florists often sell mixed bowls, but you can probably make one more cheaply using a container that you already have – and you can ring the changes with different plants.

FOLIAGE AND
FLOWERING PLANTS

MATERIALS

Bowl with drainage hole
Crocks or bark chippings
Compost
Spare pot the same size as
  centrepiece plant pot

PLANTS

Collection of mixed foliage and
flowering plants

1 Cover the drainage hole with crocks or bark chippings. Part-fill the container with compost.

2 It is a good idea to have a showy centrepiece plant – insert an empty pot temporarily so that you are sure to leave enough space.

3 Place the other plants around the centrepiece, rearranging them as necessary while still in their pots. Do not start planting until you are happy with the results.

GARDENER'S TIP

For a lively, varied mix use a combination of small bushy, vertical, and trailing plants. Tradescantias are a good choice for the last category, particularly since they come in a wide range of bright colours, including greens, creams and bronze.

PLANT AT ANY TIME OF YEAR

4 Remove the plants from their pots and plant. Finally, insert the centrepiece. If it is likely to be a long-term occupant, remove it from its pot. If you are likely to have to replace it after a few weeks – as is common with flowering plants once they finish blooming – keep it in its container.

Start a Collection

Once houseplants become more of a consuming hobby than a passing pleasure, you will begin to look for more ways to feed your passion. One option is to start a collection of a particular type of plants, whether a large and diverse group such as cacti, or a smaller, interesting group like saintpaulias (African violets).

SAINTPAULIAS

MATERIALS

Baskets or containers of various sizes
Florist's foam
Moss

PLANTS

Collection of plants, such as saintpaulias (African violets)

1 Start by grouping your plants to find an arrangement that pleases you.

2 The design will look more interesting if you can create a cascade effect using florist's foam to build up different levels.

3 Build up the back of the display on florist's foam first.

4 Fill in the space in front in steps. Try the plants for size so that you can use more foam beneath the pots if needed.

5 Arrange the plants to look as though they could be growing as a natural group and not in straight rows. Fill the spaces between the pots with moss.

GARDENER'S TIP

To find the best range of plants, do not rely on the average garden centre. You must hunt out a specialist nursery where they will have a far more imaginative and superior collection: everything to satisfy the enthusiast.

PLANT IN EARLY SPRING

Orchid Basket

MILTONIA

PLANTS

Miltonia or phalaenopsis orchid

Orchids are no longer the rare exotic plants that they used to be and most garden centres now stock some. A few inexpensive materials and a little time will create a stylish container to show these lovely flowers at their very best.

MATERIALS

Plastic-lined twig basket, 15 cm (6 in) diameter
Gravel
Sphagnum moss
3 x 40 cm (16 in) canes
Raffia

1 Pour a 2.5 cm (1 in) layer of gravel into the base of the basket and line with moss.

2 Slip the orchid (still in its pot) into the basket.

3 Push the canes into the moss at the edge of the basket so that they are held firmly in place.

4 Tie a length of raffia between each cane, finishing off with a neat knot.

GARDENER'S TIP

Orchids do not like to stand in water, but they do like a humid atmosphere. A layer of gravel underneath the pot acts as a reservoir for excess water which creates humidity. The orchid will also benefit from being sprayed with water.

PLANT AT ANY TIME OF THE YEAR

Plant Crazy

These highly decorative and unusual planters are enhanced by the careful choice of plants which provide the royal head-dresses. The queen's tresses float delicately above the crown, whilst the king's tumble downwards.

MATERIALS

2 decorative pots
Gravel
Compost

PLANTS

Chandelier plant
(Kalanchoe
tubiflora)
Creeping fig
(Ficus pumila)

CREEPING FIG

CHANDELIER
PLANT

1 Pour a 5 cm (2 in) layer of gravel into the bottom of the pots.

2 Place the chandelier plant into the planter; if there is any space around the rootball, fill with compost and gently firm the plant in position.

3 After you have planted the creeping fig in the other planter, arrange the sprays of leaves so that they resemble hair. As the plant grows it will need an occasional haircut to keep it under control. Water regularly and stand in a light position.

GARDENER'S TIP

If you are going away for a few days during the summer months, give your houseplants a holiday in the garden. Stand them on a tray lined with a thick layer of damp newspaper, positioned in a shady corner, where they will not dry out.

PLANT AT ANY TIME
OF THE YEAR

Period Fuchsias

Fuchsias were first cultivated in Europe in the 1780s. Many cultivars bred in the 1800s can still be found in cultivation today. Fuchsia 'Bland's New Striped' was first seen in cultivation in 1872, and 'Claire de Lune' in 1880. Growing plants from a particular period will add an exciting historic flavour to any collection.

MATERIALS

Victorian copper pot
Expanded clay granules
Victorian-style planter
Crocks
Compost

PLANTS

Fuchsia *'Claire de Lune'*
Fuchsia *'Bland's New Striped'*

1 Put a layer of expanded clay granules into the base of the Victorian copper pot. This will help to create a humid atmosphere around the plants.

2 Place the *Fuchsia* 'Claire de Lune' in the copper pot, arranging the branches and foliage to fall around the sides.

3 Cover the drainage hole in the bottom of the Victorian-style planter with terracotta crocks.

4 Fill the pot with compost.

5 Remove *F.* 'Bland's New Striped' from its pot. The network of fresh, healthy roots shows that the plant is strong and vigorous.

6 Plant in the compost. Cover the rootball and firm the compost with your hands.

GARDENER'S TIP

Orange flowers are often considered to be a modern advance in fuchsia cultivars, but 'Lye's Unique' has salmon-orange flowers, and originated in 1886. Other old varieties to look out for include 'Charming', a hardy bush which was developed in 1877.

PLANT IN EARLY SPRING OR EARLY SUMMER

Copper-bottomed Begonia

The stunningly marked leaves of this begonia are shown to great advantage in this old copper pot. The pot was an inexpensive purchase from a flea market, and was cleaned before use.

MATERIALS

Copper pot, 20 cm (8 in) diameter
Lemon
Slow-release plant food granules
Clay granules

PLANT

Begonia

BEGONIA

1 Rub the tarnished pot with half a lemon. The acidity of the juice will quickly clean the pot, but don't overclean it or it will look brand new and lose some of its character.

2 Place the begonia, in its plastic pot, in the copper container. Scatter a teaspoon of plant food granules on the surface of the compost.

3 Surround the plant with clay granules. Place in a light, but not sunny, position and water regularly.

GARDENER'S TIP

Other houseplants recommended for this treatment are streptocarpus, gynura and cyclamen.

PLANT AT ANY TIME OF THE YEAR

Dramatic Datura

The angel's trumpet or *Datura* (strictly speaking, it should now be known as *Brugmansia*), a popular conservatory plant, will grow enormous in time, provided it is planted in a large container and given regular food and water. The plant will benefit from a period outdoors during the summer, but will grow indoors for the rest of the year.

MATERIALS

Deep planter, at least 40 cm (16 in) diameter
Polystyrene or similar drainage material
Gloves
Equal mix loam-based compost and container compost
Slow-release plant food granules

PLANTS

Angel's trumpet (Brugmansia suaveolens)
4 white busy lizzies (impatiens)

ANGEL'S TRUMPET

BUSY LIZZIE

1 Fill the base of the container with lightweight polystyrene or similar drainage material. Wear gloves to lift the angel's trumpet into the container.

2 Pour compost round the edges of the plant, pressing down firmly around the rootball. Scatter 2 tablespoons of plant food granules on the surface.

3 Plant the busy Lizzies around the base of the angel's trumpet, and remember to water frequently.

GARDENER'S TIP

All parts of the angel's trumpet are poisonous, and it should be handled with care. Standing it outside in summer is recommended as the scent of the flowers can have a narcotic effect in confined spaces. It is not recommended in households with small children. While it is sensible to be cautious, it is also a fact that many commonly cultivated plants are poisonous. For example, with the exception of its tubers, the potato plant is poisonous, as are dieffenbachia and oleander.

PLANT IN SPRING

Plant Guide

Anemone blanda
Aquilegia alpina
Arabis ferdinandi-
   coburgii 'Variegata'
Asplenium crispum
Athyrium nipponicum
Berberis thunbergii
   'Atropurpurea Nana',
   B. darwinii
Bergenia
Box
Ceratostigma
   plumbagoides
Chamaecyparis pisifera
   'Filifera Aurea,
   'Sungold'
Choisya ternata
Convolvulus cneorum
Cotoneaster conspicuus
Crocus
Day lily
Dianthus
Dryopteris filix-mas
Euonymous fortunei
   'Emerald and Gold'
Euphorbia
Foxglove
Hebe
Helianthemum
Heuchera 'Palace
   Purple', 'Bressingham
   Bronze'

Holly
Hosta
Hydrangea
Inula
Iris reticulata
Ivy
Lamium
Lavender
Lily-of-the-valley
Narcissus
Nepeta mussinii
Ophiopogon planiscapus
   'Nigrescens'
Pachysandra terminalis
Polygonum affine
Polystichum
   acrostichoides
Potentilla
Primula auricula
Rosemary
Salix alpina
Sedum 'Ruby Glow'
Sedum ewersii
Sempervivum
Skimmia japonica
   'Rubella'
Thyme
Trachelospermum
   jasminoides
Veronica peduncularis
Vinca minor

TREES AND SHRUBS
FOR CONTAINERS

Acer palmatum
Apple (dwarf)
Bay
Berberis thunbergii
   'Atropurpurea Nana',
   B. darwinii
Box
Camellia
Ceratostigma
   plumbagoides
Chamaecyparis pisifera
Choisya ternata
Citrus mitis*
Convolvulus cneorum
Cordyline*
Cotoneaster conspicuus
Datura*
Euonymous fortunei
Fuchsia
Hebe
Holly
Hydrangea
Lantana*
Lavender
Potentilla
Rhododendron
Rosemary
Rose
Skimmia

CLIMBERS FOR
CONTAINERS

Bougainvillea*
Clematis alpina, C.
   macropetala
Cobaea scandens*
Gynura*
Ivy
Jasmine
Stephanotis*
Thunbergia alata
Trachelospermum
   jasminoides

TRAILING PLANTS
FOR HANGING BASKETS

Ageratum*
Begonia semperflorens*
Bidens ferulifolia*
Brachycome iberidifolia
Campanula isophylla*
Chaenorhinum
   glareosum*
Convolvulus sabatius*
Erigeron mucronatus
Felicia*
Fuchsia (lax varieties)*
Gazania*
Glechoma hederacea
Helichrysum petiolare*

Lampranthus*
Lantana*
Lobelia*
Lotus berthelotti*
Lysimachia nummularia
Nasturtium
Osteospermum*
Pelargonium*
Petunia*
Sedum ewersii
Senecio maritima*
Sweet peas
Verbena*
Vinca minor

SPRING-FLOWERING
PLANTS FOR CONTAINERS

Anagallis
Anemone blanda
Aquilegia
Arabis ferdinandi-
   coburgii 'Variegata'
Bluebells
Crocus
Day lily
Euphorbia
Forget-me-not
Iris reticulata

Lily-of-the-valley
Narcissus
Polyanthus
Primroses
Primula auricula
Snowdrops
Tulips
Vinca minor
Viola
Wallflower

AUTUMN AND
WINTER COLOUR

Arabis ferdinandi-
   coburgii 'Variegata'
Berberis thunbergii
   'Atropurpurea Nana',
   B. darwinii
Bergenia
Ceratostigma
   plumbagoides
Chamaecyparis pisifera
   'Sungold'
Convolvulus cneorum
Euonymous fortunei
Euphorbia
Ferns
Heuchera 'Palace
   Purple', 'Bressingham
   Bronze'
Hakonechloa macra
   'Alboaurea'
Hebe
Holly
Iris unguicularis
Ivy
Pachysandra terminalis
Polygonum affine
Salvia greggii
Sedum 'Ruby Glow'
Vinca minor

*All plants marked with an asterisk need protection from frost

PLANTS FOR SHADE

Anemone blanda
Begonia semperflorens
Bergenia
Box
Campanula isophylla
Chamaecyparis pisifera
Digitalis
Euonymous
Euphorbia
Ferns
Glechoma hederacea
Heuchera
Holly
Hosta
Hydrangea
Impatiens*
Ivy
Lily-of-the-valley
Narcissus
Ophiopogon planiscapus
Pachysandra terminalis
Primrose
Primula auricula
Skimmia
Sorrel
Thunbergia alata
Trachelospermum
 jasminoides
Vinca minor
Viola

PLANTS FOR HOT CONDITIONS

Aloe*
Alyssum
Argyranthemum*
Arundinaria pygmaea
Crassula ovata*
Diascia*
Erigeron mucronatus*
Gazania*
Hakonechloa macra
 'Aureola'
Helianthemum
Inula
Lavender
Lotus berthelotti*
Mesembryanthemum*
Osteospermum*

PLANTS WITH DECORATIVE FOLIAGE

Berberis thunbergii
Bergenia
Chamaecyparis pisifera
Choisya ternata
Convolvulus cneorum
Euonymous fortunei
Euphorbia
Fuchsia magellanica
Glechoma hederacea
Hebe
Hedera helix 'Hibernica'
Helichrysum petiolare*
Heuchera
Holly
Hosta 'Blue Moon'
Lotus berthelotti*
Lysimachia nummularia
Nasturtium 'Alaska'
Pachysandra terminalis
Pelargonium, ivy-leaved
Salvia officinalis
Senecio maritima
Thymus 'Silver Queen',
 'Archer's gold'
Vinca minor

FRAGRANT PLANTS

Alyssum
Bidens atrosanguinea*
Cheiranthus
Choisya ternata
Citrus mitis*
Dianthus
Heliotrope
Jasmine
Lavender
Lilies
Lily-of-the-valley
Nicotiana
Pelargonium, scented-
 leaved varieties*
Rosemary
Sweet pea
Thyme
Trachelospermum
 jasminoides
Viola odorata

Index

Index

ACKNOWLEDGEMENTS

All projects were created by Stephanie Donaldson and photographed by Marie O'Hara unless stated below.

Contributors
Clare Bradley: pp 215, 219, 220, 221, 222, 223, 224, 226, 227, 230, 231. Blaise Cooke: pp 12, 13, 34, 40l, 43br, 58, 72, 73, 199, 202, 208, 209, 225, 246, 247. Tessa Evelegh: pp 8-9, 20, 26t, 29, 30t, 32t, 32m, 33, 35, 36, 38, 39, 43t. Peter McHoy: pp 32, 37, 40r, 227, 229, 230, 231, 238, 239, 240, 241, 242, 243. Lesley Harle: p 44. Karin Hossack: pp 45, 46. Liz Wagstaff: p 47, 48.

Photographers
John Freeman: pp 2, 3, 5, 12, 13, 14, 17r, 20m, 20b, 21b, 22r, 23mr, 26m, 28, 34, 42tl, 43br, 58, 72, 73, 101, 102, 103, 105, 106, 107, 108, 109, 120, 128, 132, 133, 136, 137, 140, 141, 142, 143, 144, 145, 147, 148, 153, 158, 159, 161, 167, 174, 175, 193, 194, 195, 199, 202, 204, 205, 206, 207, 208, 209, 210, 211, 215, 219, 220, 221, 222, 223, 224, 225, 226, 227, 232, 233, 235, 236, 237, 243, 244, 245, 246, 247, 248, 249. Don Last: p 19r, 229, 230, 231, 238, 239, 240, 241, 242, 243. Debbie Patterson: pp 8-9, 20m, 20b, 21b, 22l, 26t, 29, 30t, 32t, 32m, 33, 35, 38, 39, 43, 44, 45, 46, 47, 48, 59. Peter McHoy: pp 18, 19l, 27, 32, 37, 40r.

t=top, b=bottom, m=middle, l=left, r=right

NOTES

NOTES

NOTES

NOTES

NOTES

NOTES

NOTES

NOTES